# Group Lessons
## for Suzuki® Violin and Viola
## by Carolyn McCall

© 1993 Summy-Birchard Music
division of Summy-Birchard Inc.
All rights reserved    Printed in U.S.A.

Summy-Birchard Inc.
exclusively distributed by
Warner Bros. Publications
15800 N.W. 48th Avenue, Miami, FL 33014

The Suzuki name, logo and wheel device
are trademarks of Dr. Shinichi Suzuki used
under exclusive license by Summy-Birchard, Inc.

Any duplication, adaptation or arrangement of the compositions
contained in this collection requires the written consent of the Publisher.
No part of this book may be photocopied or reproduced in any way without permission.
Unauthorized uses are an infringement of the U.S. Copyright Act and are punishable by law.

**CAROLYN McCALL** (formerly Meyer) has been a Suzuki student, parent, and teacher. She received her B.A. in music from the University of Illinois and her M.M. in violin performance from the Southern Illinois University at Edwardsville. She has lived and taught in Austria, Wisconsin, and Illinois. She currently teaches violin, viola, and music and movement through SIUE and at workshops and institutes. She is the author of many articles in addition to this book.

# *FOREWORD*

I am the organizer, not the originator, of most of the ideas in this book. This work is a compilation of repertory group lesson ideas from many sources. It is difficult to trace their origins.

However, special recognition must go to John Kendall, with whom I did the majority of my Suzuki teacher training. I have also learned a tremendous amount from classes at workshops, conferences, and institutes (in particular the American Suzuki Institute at Stevens Point, Wisconsin). *The American Suzuki Journal* and *Suzuki World* magazines have been wonderful sources of ideas over the years. Two books (William Starr's *The Suzuki Violinist* and Kay Collier Slone's *They're Rarely Too Young and Seldom Too Old to Twinkle*) have been invaluable.

Ultimately I owe my fascination with string teaching to Shinichi Suzuki, whose philosophy enriches all of our lives.

Thanks to all who have shared in the past and will share in the future!

*In memory of Grammie, who loved to teach, and Papa, who loved to sing.*

# TABLE
# OF
# CONTENTS

# TABLE OF CONTENTS

*Concentration and Coordination*
    1. Hand and Feet Labels
    2. Memory Games
    3. Identification Games
    4. Concentrating Amid Difficulties
    5. Focal Points
    6. Imitation
    7. Antiphony
    8. Separate the Hands
    9. New Twinkles
*Right Hand Techniques*
    1. Basic Down and Up, With Articulations
    2. Bow Arm
    3. Tone
*Left Hand Techniques*
    1. Block, Prepared, or Independent Fingering
    2. Finger Patterns
*Musicality*
    1. Dynamics
    2. Ensemble Skills
    3. Exaggerate What Is Different
*Combined Violin And Viola Groups*
*Central Themes*
*End Of Lesson*

# TABLE OF CONTENTS

# TABLE OF CONTENTS

# INTRODUCTION

Many students presently study violin and viola via the Suzuki approach. These students generally have weekly individual lessons on their instruments, and the relationship between the Suzuki student, parent, and teacher is often described as a triangle.

Three additional aspects of learning via the Suzuki approach form another triangle:

*home practice*

*individual lesson*          *group lesson*

Suzuki students are pooled together into a wide variety of group repertory and music reading lessons. Some lessons include only students of like ages and ability levels; others merge students of many levels. A teacher may be asked to work with a small or a huge number of students at one time. The availability and expertise of assisting parents, teachers and piano accompanists varies as much as the teaching situations.

Group lessons also vary in their long- or short-term duration. Some groups of students will receive instruction from the same teacher regularly for a long time, while other groups are created only for a specific workshop or institute. Primary purposes for group instruction include: ensemble, inspiration, polishing, and performance. Group lessons motivate both students and parents and are a good source of social interaction and support.

Playing fundamentals and the students' growing repertories and musical awareness form the basis of group lesson content. The students build their technique with pieces they can play. An important part of each student's review is the musicality he can bring to his pieces. The group lesson provides an opportunity to absorb new and different but still acceptable musical ideas.

This book is a compilation of violin and viola repertory group lesson ideas from many sources, planned to reinforce what is learned at individual lessons and at home. These ideas are based on the premise that no one but the accompanist uses sheet music during the lesson. The book is organized according to students' ability levels, pre-Twinkle through Book 4. Each chapter contains an introduction, suggested warm-up activities, and appropriate ideas for working toward the following general goals:

   (Note: this does not represent the order of a lesson)
   - posture
   - concentration and coordination
   - right hand techniques (including tone)
   - left hand techniques
   - musicality

Activities for combined violin and viola groups, possible central themes, and suggestions for the end of the group lesson wrap up each section of the book.

# CHAPTER ONE:
## *PRE-TWINKLE*

*INTRODUCTION*

Parents are vital pre-Twinkle group lesson participants. As long as the children are in the lesson room, they will be absorbing lesson ideas. If a student cannot handle being a part of the group, he should sit quietly on the "sidelines" with his parent. With variety in their group lesson, many pre-Twinklers can last for a 45-minute session.

One basic pre-Twinkle group set-up is made by marking out a circle of masking tape spots in the center of the room. Each student chooses a piece of masking tape to sit on, and his parent sits behind him. For safety's sake, (pre-)instruments and bows should be kept in their open cases, within easy reach. It is a nice touch to have a recording of Book One softly playing in the background before the lesson begins. Always begin the lesson on time; this will encourage punctuality the next time.

Along with any necessary name introductions, a sentence or two to each of the students noticing something special (such as their apparel) makes them feel more comfortable. Admire new cases and instruments. Keep announcement-making to the absolute minimum. The students are psyched up to start learning, and this momentum should not be lost.

Many teachers begin and end each lesson with a respectful bow. The teacher bows to the class, and the class bows together to the teacher.

*POSTURE*

### 1. Feet

Pre-Twinkle posture-learning begins with the feet. If the students have not already received *foot-charts* (or something with proper foot placement marked on it), make charts on file folders or pizza circles at the first group session:

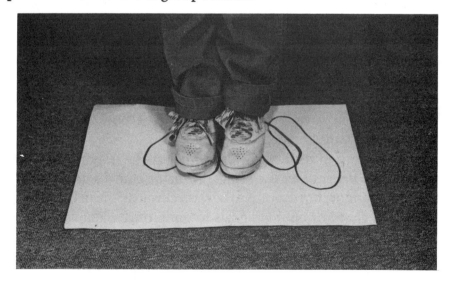

Eventually the students should be capable of the proper foot placement without any visual aids. Measure the *width of their shoulders* with a bow or measuring stick; then check to see whether their feet are shoulder-width apart in playing position.

Activities to reinforce proper foot posture include:

1. Pretend the students are *trees*. Scoop up "dirt" from the floor and "plant" their roots by patting the "dirt" on their feet. This encourages solid feet. Make a "woo-ooo" sound like a big wind; this wind may sway the "trees" (gently sway the students to check that their knees are not locked), but it will not knock the "trees" over.

2. See how quickly the students can *go back and forth* from rest position feet to V-feet to playing position feet. Throw in some other variations such as T-feet or L-feet! (Very young pre-Twinklers may need to set their rest position feet slightly apart for better balance.) Some teachers have the students *step back* with the right foot to achieve playing position feet. This keeps the body weight properly on the left foot.

## 2. Taking a Bow

One of the first things beginners learn to do is to *take a bow*. The group can learn to bow together in unison. They must put their feet into rest position, place their hands at their sides (or later hold instrument and bow in rest position), and bow from the waist before straightening up once again. Experiment with bows that are too little ("baby" bows), too big ("giant" bows), and just right.

Use a phrase to help the students have the same duration to their bows; "Down Two, Up Two" helps keep the group together. A "magic" word whispered in each ear captures their attention. They think this word when they bow and straighten up together. Compound words such as "toaster-oven" and "flowerpot" are of good bowing length.

If a piano is in the room, someone can *play a chord* to signal the bow. (A major is best for beginning violins; D major for violists. These are the tonic keys of their first few pieces, and at later groups they will bow to tonic chords). It helps the pianist to know when to play the chord if the teacher starts a very slight nod first. Some accompanists play a dominant seventh chord to signal everyone to prepare for bowing and then play a tonic chord for the actual bow. Bows are most attractive if a *smile* is added at the end.

If a piano is available, teach the students to respond to certain signals with *things other than bows*. A major chord signals them to bow, and a minor chord means to bow "backwards" (lean backwards). A staccato chord or chords signals to jump once or however many times there were chords; an arpeggiated chord means to wiggle. As soon as the piano stops its notes, the students should stop moving.

### 3. Violin or Viola Hold

Pre-Twinklers initially use *boxes* instead of instruments. The box is the same height as the proper-sized instrument for each child and has a sponge attached just as the instrument will. At the group lesson, parents see that children of various body types, tensions, and degrees of cooperation can all learn.

First the students learn to put their instruments in *rest position*. They get lots of practice correctly placing the box (or instrument) during group drills. Pat the student's right side just before he puts the instrument into rest position. Have them pick their boxes or real instruments up from a variety of turnings on the floor:

-scroll to the left (easiest)
-scroll to the right
-scroll pointing ahead or behind the student
-instrument behind the student

The student should always use his left hand to pick up the instrument by its neck. The right arm gently hugs the instrument to the body. If the arm is just behind the fine tuners, the tuners will not get caught in a sweater.

After the students get their feet into playing position, the parents set the boxes on the children's *shoulders*. Each adult should be situated to his child's left, with the child's playing position foot pointing towards the adult. Keeping instruments high is encouraged by bringing the instrument to the student's shoulder from a point higher in the air. Each child should learn to keep both shoulders relaxed while turning the head to the left and dropping it onto the box (or instrument). Check that students are not hunching their left shoulders. Have them try holding their instruments in playing position with left hands:

-on right shoulders, under right armpits, or at right waists
-on the instruments' right shoulders
-in first position (after they learn to set their left hands)

The students can experience how heavy their *heads* are. The teacher lies on her back on the floor and gives each a turn at gently lifting her head up off the floor and carefully setting it back again. They will feel the actual heaviness of a head. They can try lifting each others' heads. Take the opportunity to interject a statement about how a heavy head can easily hold up a violin or viola.

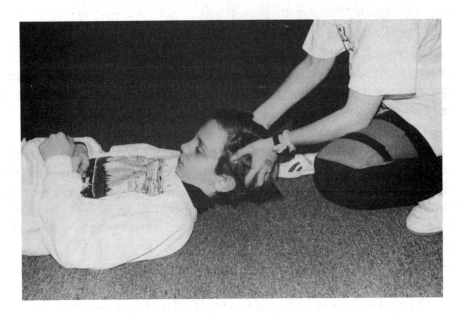

In a group of four or less, quickly set each box in playing position and see how *long* the students can hold them there. (In a larger group the parents and teacher should set all of the boxes at once so that the students do not have to wait too long.) Some ideas for stretching the playing position time include having the teacher:

1. Count to some number
   (at high speed or in a foreign language if variety is needed)
2. Tell a short story
3. Sing a (Suzuki) song
4. Say a tongue twister
5. Set a 1-minute timer
6. Lead a parade of playing positions around the room

Eventually the *students* may try setting the boxes or the instruments with less and less help from parents or teacher. Keep reinforcing what landmarks to watch for, such as *"nose, bridge, elbow, toes"*. (The student's nose points to the bridge of the instrument, which is over the left elbow, which is over the left foot.) Finally, the students learn to put their instruments from playing position back to rest position alone.

Generally the instrument is set with its left side on the *shoulder seam of the student's shirt.* Have the students discover where their own as well as their parents' shoulder seams are.

Another way for a small group to work on posture is for the teacher to hold her own instrument incorrectly and have the students take turns being the "*detective*" and figuring out what is incorrect.

Once the students have learned to set their instruments on their shoulders correctly, play quickness games such as "*On your mark, get set, GO!*" The teacher has her back to the students while saying this, and they pick their instruments up from the floor and put them into playing position as quickly as they can. They should put their instruments up only after the word "GO"; if the teacher occasionally substitutes words for "GO", they should not react.

To check that the instruments are being held securely by the weight of the students' heads, *tug* gently on each instrument's scroll. Place a small object (marble, peanut, piece of candy) in their instruments' pegboxes. If the instruments stay up correctly, the objects stay put.

Once their playing positions are secure, the students are more eager than ever to play those instruments. One last way to hold off premature playing is to teach the group basic right-hand *pizzicato.* They can get some satisfaction plucking the open strings of their instruments. After anchoring their right thumbs towards the end of their fingerboards, the students pluck with their index fingers. A piano accompanist can improvise some staccato chords which harmonize with the open strings of the student's instruments.

When the students can play a "Twinkle" variation, check the stability of their postures by having them *wave at or shake left hands* with partners (other students, or parents) while playing the open strings of the piece.

## 4. Bow Hold

It is important that families learn to follow careful guidelines from the start. Establishing good habits is easier than doing remedial work later. Beginners should not be allowed to play instruments before good posture habits are firmly established.

Young students first need to gain a little control of how to *tense and relax* their bow hands. Have each make his hand "hard like a rock" or "soft like a marshmallow".

Show the students and parents how to make soft, round "*rabbits*" with their bow hands. Keep the middle fingers down over the nail of the bent thumb while relaxing the "ears" (outer fingers). Have the "rabbits" hop around, eat lettuce, get on airplanes and fly, etc.

The "rabbits" turn into "*butterflies*" as the students shake out their

bow hands. Challenge them to go back and forth quickly from "rabbits" to "butterflies". Finally the "butterflies" rest on a parent's outstretched index finger or the right end of a (pre-)bow. (3/4" dowel sticks cut to 18" lengths make good pre-bows.)

Turn the "butterflies" into "*monkey tails*"; the students feel a hanging feeling in their bow hands as they hang from an outstretched finger or stick. Set right thumbs in the proper early bow hold (on the outside of the frog, usually across from the middle finger). Push the fourth finger up until it is perched on top, and tilt the (pre-)bow tip to point up. If necessary, insert a small foam ball in the palm of the bow hand to encourage a round, relaxed feeling.

After the early bow hold has been established on a (pre-)bow, the student needs to build *endurance* for holding it that way. Perhaps he and his parent also need motivation to keep working carefully at such a detailed operation. The teacher can demonstrate to the group how messy her printing becomes if she does not hold a pencil correctly. An instrument also sounds messy when the player does not hold the bow correctly.

To pass the time while developing bow-hold endurance, use similar activities to those for instrument-hold endurance. Try the following poem with actions:
"Up like a rocket,
Down like the rain.
Back and forth like a choo-choo train.
Round and round like a great big sun-
Bow on my hand; curved pinkie, bent thumb!"

Bow hold endurance can also be built through *stirring soup*: each member of a small group adds one more imaginary ingredient to the soup, which everyone is stirring in front of themselves with their bow tips pointing toward the ceiling. This makes a good memory game when each must name the previous soup ingredients in their correct order before adding his own ingredient. The students can also draw *different-sized circles* in the air: cheerios; cookies; pancakes; pizza; etc. They are actually drawing three circles at once: one with the frog of the bow; another with the tip; and a third with the right elbow. Slightly older pre-Twinklers can *write their names* in the air with their bows. Test their bow-hold stability by having them pass their bows up and down through horizontal *canning jar screw bands* or circles parents make with their hands. The object of this activity is to get the bow up and down through the circle without touching the sides or receiving help from the left hand.

Yet another endurance-builder is *rocket ships*. The students hold their bows ("rockets") vertically on some designated launching pad such as the floor or their knees. The teacher says "3-2-1-SLOW BLASTOFF!" (By saying "slow blastoff", a lot of wildness is avoided.)

14

The rockets go up to the moon, and back down again.

*Windshield wipers* tests a strong fourth finger. Hold the bow with the tip pointing up, and then tip it to the left until it is parallel to the floor. Then tip it to the right until it is parallel to the floor. Try to do this by rotating the forearm only.

To clarify what is correct, the teacher holds her bow incorrectly. The students (in a small group) take turns being the "*detective*" and figuring out how to fix the problems.

Teachers and parents can give *bow-hold shake tests.* The students hold their bows with the tips pointing up, and the adults grasp the tips of the bows and gently shake them.

*CONCENTRATION AND COORDINATION*

## 1. Hand and Feet Labels

Draw a small violin (or viola) on the back of each student's left hand and a small bow on the right hand. Give the parents pens so that they can try drawing similar pictures on the backs of their own hands. (Some children may have been scolded in the past for drawing on themselves. Reassure them that these pictures will disappear when the hands are washed.) They all hide their hands behind their backs, and the teacher calls out, "Violin (or viola) hand!" They each bring a hand around and check to see that this hand has a picture of an instrument on it. They quickly hide their hands again, and the teacher calls out, "Bow hand!" If some are having trouble, call out the same command a few times in a row. At the next class, see if the students know which hand is which without the aid of the pictures.

When playing an instrument, the hands must learn to do *different things* at the same time. Lead the following activities:

-Rub tummies and pat heads (or vice-versa) at the same time
-Do circles in the air in opposite directions with index fingers
-Touch one hand to the nose, and cross arms so the other hand can touch an ear. Then- reverse the hands!

## 2. Finger Numbers

To reinforce string finger numbers, sing a version of "*Where Is Thumbkin?*" (tune: "Are You Sleeping?"):
(Hide hands behind backs.)
    "Where's Mr. First Finger? Where's Mr. First Finger?"
(Bring out first one hand with index finger extended, then other.)
    "Here I am! -Here I am!"
(Tap index finger and thumb together.)
    "How are you today, Sir? -Very well, I thank you!"
(Hide first one hand and then the other behind back again.)
    "Run away. Run away."

Vary the finger numbers as well as their sexes. For example:
    Mrs. Second Finger (Bring out both first and second finger.)
    Ms. Third Finger
    Mr. Bent Thumb (bow hand)
    Mr. Banana Thumb (left hand- it's slightly curved and soft, like a banana)
*Tap* the finger being sung about against the thumb; watch that the students are making circles with their fingers and thumbs when they tap. This exercises the knuckle action necessary for string playing.

Another *finger number drill* begins with all participants hiding their hands behind their backs. A leader says, "First finger!", and everyone brings their first fingers around in front as fast as they can and then quickly puts them back. Speed up the tempo of the game.

Even though these students are not yet playing their instruments, they should become aware of the eventual need to keep their fingernails short. A *nail check* will serve this purpose; loan the parents nailclippers to use as needed.

## 3. Parts of the Instrument

New Suzuki families will become more comfortable handling and caring for their instruments if they know more about them. The teacher can use her own instrument as a model if the students are still learning on boxes. Young pre-Twinklers can count pegs, strings, and fine tuners. Point out a few more *parts of the instrument* at each group session, and assign the students to draw pictures of real instruments and bows at home. Once the students use real instruments, help them look inside with a small flashlight to learn how old each instrument in the group is. A violin or viola can be compared to the human body: both have a neck and shoulders as well as a chin, ears, and cheeks. Point out that the students will eventually use bigger instruments as their bodies grow. This plants the image of the children playing violin or viola throughout their lives.

Labelling the parts of the instrument is a convenient lead-in to discussing how to take *care of the instrument.* Show the students how to rosin their bows, and let them polish their instruments with a treated cloth. The group lesson is a good place to reinforce safety rules such as:

1. Allow only the student, parent, and teacher to handle the instrument or bow.

2. Keep the instrument in one of three places: in the case; in rest position; or in playing position.

3. Keep fingers away from bow hair.

4. Do not chew on the scroll, pegs, or bow tip.

5. Do not grind the tip of the bow into the floor.

## 4. Memory Games

In addition to *stirring soup* to practice bow holds, other games will help students develop their memories. *Number sequence games* are good for all ages. A leader says a number, and the group repeats it in rhythm. The leader repeats the first number and adds another, and the group repeats all of this in rhythm. The game goes on until the group begins to stumble. Putting a sequence of numbers into this game makes it easier.

Another memory game is to *label some body parts with numbers.* For example:

1 = head    2 = shoulders    3 = waist    4 = knees

The teacher quickly calls out numbers and touches her corresponding body parts. The students follow as best they can.

See if the group can retain the *memory of a pitch.* The pitch of the open A string is good to work on for future tuning needs and provides an opportunity to demonstrate the use of a tuning fork. The students match a pitch, have their attention drawn elsewhere, and then try to recall the pitch.

## 5. Identification Games

Pre-Twinklers and their parents learn a lot about where they are headed through identification games. Ideas include:

*Name that tune or rhythm-* Play a "Twinkle" rhythm or the beginning of an early piece, and have the students identify it.

*Sections of Twinkle-* Label the sections of "Twinkle" (for example:

Bread/Baloney/Baloney/Bread- cardboard models may help).

1. Play a section for the group or certain individuals to identify. (Play the sample section very quickly: "Super Twinkle"! Otherwise, the part of the Bread section which is like the Baloney section may confuse the students.)

2. Have the students and parents form two circles; one moves around only to Bread and the other only to Baloney.

3. Have the students and parents form one big circle which moves to the right to Bread and to the left for Baloney.

*String names-* With or without watching, students try to identify which open string the teacher is playing. They can also identify whether the teacher is playing *pizzicato* or *arco*.

## RIGHT HAND TECHNIQUES

### 1. Basic Down and Up

The parents must thoroughly understand the *motions* of the "Twinkle" rhythms. When a group sings "Twinkle", teach the rudimentary feeling of down-bow and up-bow. Everyone stands to sing, and their *bodies go down or up* (bending/straightening their knees) with each syllable, just as the instrument's bow goes down or up with each note. Parents and students typically get caught on the longer notes such as "star"; they try to go down and then up again with the beat instead of staying down on the longer note.

Parents and students can *shake bow hands* to the various "Twinkle" rhythms. Have the students take turns *rolling a small toy car* down and up a surface to the rhythms. Have the parents draw the rhythms with down and up strokes over their children's *spines*. Each rhythm starts down. (Variation B alternates by starting down on the first pitch and up on the next pitch.) Some names that are often used for the rhythms include:

Var. A | Mississippi Hot Dog/ Goody Goody Quick Quick/ Mississippi River/Gravy and Potatoes/ I Like Choc'late Ice-Cream/Mississippi Stop Stop/ Manitoba Hot Dog/ Charlie Brown and Snoopy

Var. B    Yo-ka-ta/(2-syllable name), I'm [Andy, I'm Andy, etc.] / Peanuts, and Popcorn/Doctor Suzuki says never be lazy: just practice and practice until you go crazy!

Var. C    Stop Pony, Stop Pony/ Run Mother, Run Father/ Jack Rabbit Eats Carrots, Down Wiggle, Up Wiggle

Var. D    Mississippi Is a River/ Mississippi Huckelberry/(2-syllable name) Rides a Motorcycle [Grandma Rides a Motorcycle]

Make the analogy that just as a person may have different names (Mary Smith, Mrs. Smith, Mom), rhythms can have different names. The choice of labels for these rhythms will affect the bow *articulation* the student eventually uses.  For example, the Variation A label "Mississippi Stop Stop" is helpful for encouraging a comfortable legato stroke on the sixteenth notes and a crisp staccato articulation on the eighth notes.

Build awareness of these basic bow strokes before the students ever actually play the instrument. By rubbing their hands smoothly together they experience "*legato*"; rubbing the hands choppily simulates "*staccato*". They can learn to recognize these strokes in the Book One pieces they hear on their tapes.  The students can also "*draw*" the rhythms on a piece of paper.  Eventually they will bow up and down in a consistent place, but as an exercise in when to go down or up (and an exercise in roughly legato and staccato strokes), create patterns such as:

Mississippi Huckelberry     Mississippi Hot Dog

Long and short lines drawn on a paper to correspond with the long and short rhythms of the variations make the rhythmic concept clearer.  The eighth and sixteenth notes may be taught with equal bow length once the students play them on their instruments.

## 2. Bow Arm

Pre-Twinklers who do not yet play on instruments can try "*Dirty Doggie Scrub-Scrub*" on their left arms.  Stick out left arms (perhaps holding left hands with a parent), and place right hands on left elbows. On the first syllable of the song, move right hands down to wrists. On the next syllable, move back to elbows. "Dirty Doggie Scrub-Scrub" has the advantage of being the same rhythm as "Twinkle" Variation A and can be sung to the tune of "Twinkle":

"Dirty Doggie Scrub-Scrub,
Wash him in the tub-tub,
Rub-a-dub-a-dub-dub,
Dirty Doggie Scrub-Scrub."

This is an early training of the bow arm; the students are moving only their hands and forearms instead of sawing back with their upper arms.

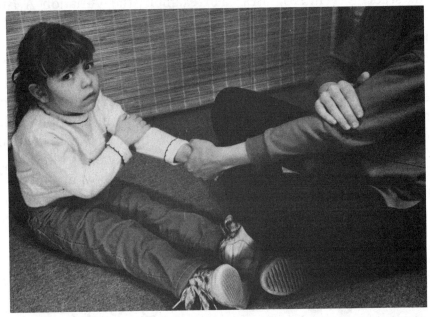

Another exercise for developing the bow arm is to bow with a (pre-) bow through an empty *toilet paper roll* held on the left shoulder by the left hand. (The toilet paper roll keeps the bow and the student's shirt cleaner.) Try "Twinkle" rhythms or early songs as appropriate.

The "square of the arm" is formed by the instrument, bow, and bow arm:

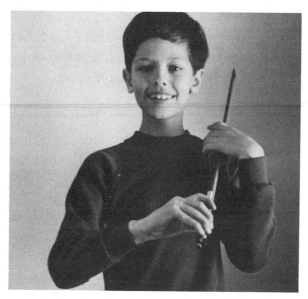

Students can play the *"Twinkle" rhythms on their appropriate open strings* at the group lesson when ready. It helps to keep nose-bridge-elbow-toes aligned if the teacher stands to the left of the playing group. Call out the name of the rhythm they are to play and add, "Ready- PLAY!" with an upward vocal inflection on "PLAY!" Repetition will be more interesting if a piano accompanist plays chords to harmonize with these open strings. One simple example is:

Students can also play "Twinkle" rhythms on an open string while the teacher and/or other students play the actual variations.

Have the students form a *"Twinkle Train"* by following a leader as they play. In a large group, divide the students into two or more trains which wind around the available space.

### 3. Tone

From the earliest pre-Twinkle stage, it is important for the student to begin to develop an ideal of violin or viola tone. Hearing the Suzuki recording on quality equipment, listening to other recordings featuring violin or viola, and watching live performances will build this concept of what the instrument should sound like.

*LEFT HAND TECHNIQUES*

### 1. Wrist

Young students need to discriminate between a straight and a crooked wrist. If their left upper arm and hand look like a hooked candycane, they are set approximately for playing the violin or viola. If the hand is bent either way from the wrist, the posture on the instrument is incorrect. Have the students close their eyes and try to determine by touch whether their parents' or teacher's "candycanes" are straight or crooked. The students will then become more aware of their own postures.

### 2. Hand

When the private teacher deems the student ready, she will begin to set up the left hand posture. Reinforce this at the group lesson by having the students learn to recognize and applaud good left-hand posture:

-straight wrist
-thumb set on the fleshy part of the thumb, approximately across from the first finger tape. (Tap the thumb several times to check that it is in the best spot for that particular hand.) The left thumb should be relaxed and soft and shaped somewhat like a banana.
-base of the first finger lightly touching the black fingerboard. (Draw a line at the base of everyone's first finger so that they become aware of where it is.)

### 3. Fingers

Each left finger should be lightly but firmly set on the appropriate fingerboard tape so that it becomes a little "house". A loose letter "Y" may be found in the creases of a properly-set first finger.

Another left-finger game is the *head tapping game*. Heads are very sensitive. Tap a left finger on the top of each student's and parent's head to demonstrate the amount of finger pressure needed in string playing. Then have the students tap their parents' heads, and vice versa.

*MUSICALITY*     1. Melody

Pre-Twinklers are not yet making music on their instruments, but they can make music with their *voices*. They get a good preview to playing early pieces by singing "The Monkey Song" (see below), "Twinkle", etc.

**The Monkey Song**

I'm a little    monkey climbing up a    ladder,    climbing to the top   to  pick a  green   banana.

I'm a   little   monkey climbing down the  ladder, climbing to the ground  to  eat my  green  banana!

Singing together helps settle down a wriggly preschool group. A student picks a song, and the teacher hums a comfortable starting note. Learning *how to begin* together ranges from the teacher saying, "Ready- sing!" to everyone in the group taking a simultaneous starting breath and beginning together. Let the students choose *tempi and dynamics*. Ask if they wish to sing loudly like bears or very quietly like fish; quickly like deer running or slowly like turtles plodding.

It helps inexperienced singers to *find the first pitch* if they come down to it in a falling voice from a very high note or rise up to it from a very low note. Using *rough hand signals* to show the basic high, middle, and low pitches of a melody builds an early awareness of rising and falling melodies. This will be necessary when the students eventually sound out pieces on their instruments. The melody of the Bread section of "Twinkle" can easily be done with hands: (Hand height shown here by word position)

                              Little
              Twinkle                      Star.
                                    How I
                                        wonder
                                             what you
Twinkle                                           are.


While the teacher plays an *ascending* scale on her instrument, the students gradually rise from a squatting position to standing. They go from standing to squatting during a *descending* scale.

## 2. Rhythm

A pre-Twinkle group is just beginning to experience some rhythmic divisions with their (pre-)bow strokes. It will help them and many of their parents to recognize a few basic rhythmic differences if they clap and/or move around the room to the teacher's drum beat:

eighth notes: "running" label
quarter note: "walk" label
half note: "step-hold" label
whole note: "hold that long note" label

Label the "Twinkle" Variation A "running running walk-walk" to help them feel the basic divisions of the beat. Slowly play different "Twinkle" variations for the students and parents to "find in their feet." A large, bare room will be needed for activities of this sort, and the class members may move anywhere in the room as long as they do not touch another person. When the music stops, they should freeze.

A pre-Twinkle class can also be made aware of the difference between clapping a steady beat (or pulse) and clapping the various rhythms of the song. Lead the students in gently tapping their chests in imitation of the steady pulses of their hearts. Then sing a song such as "Twinkle" or "Yankee Doodle" while keeping the "heart" beat going. The other way to clap or tap a song involves moving on each syllable, which will not always correspond with the "heart" beat. Try having half the group tap the "heart" beat while the others clap the song rhythms.

**CENTRAL THEMES**

The teacher may wish to organize the pre-Twinkle lesson time with a central theme such as:

*Parade Day* (Put on mini-parades of bow holds, instrument holds, etc. Follow a leader around the room while playing "Twinkle" rhythms.)  `

*Numbers Day* (Count how many times the students repeat certain activities. Count the sides of their squares. Play the numbers memory game.)

*Strong Muscles Day* (Point out the growing strength in the students' fingers, arms, necks, etc.)

*Five Senses Day* (Help the students think of ways in which they use their different senses to play their instruments. For "taste", try licking rosin! Be sure to point out that rosin is not edible.)

*Hands Day* (Build awareness of what different things the hands do to play an instrument.)

*Copy Cat Day* (Use a lot of imitation exercises. Speak as little as possible.)

**END OF LESSON**

The cooling-down time of a pre-Twinkle group includes activities where the students sit. They may watch each other do solos such as rosining a bow; showing an instrument playing position or bow hold; playing a rhythm on an instrument; or performing a "Twinkle" variation. *Singing or rhythmic activities* may often be done while sitting. The class ends with a supervised putting-away of instruments and bows. The teacher says she is looking forward to seeing everybody again next time.

# CHAPTER TWO:
## SUZUKI BOOK ONE

**INTRODUCTION**   Violin and viola students who can play "Twinkle" have already learned many string playing basics. Book One students begin to develop the important skill of playing well with others.

Parents should provide food and bathroom opportunities before the lesson so the children can really concentrate. Hands should be clean and fingernails trimmed. Unpack cases in a convenient corner and rosin bows as needed. Observers sit quietly and watch from near an exit. With a minimum of "noodling noise", the tuning time begins.

Some teachers like to set up a "tuning line": the children form a line at the piano and have their instruments tuned one at a time. This gives the teacher a chance to greet each child personally. It is also a good opportunity for instrument inspection. If a bridge needs to be straightened, the teacher can do so while sitting on the piano bench and can educate the students and parents about what she is doing. Other teachers prefer to place the students into class rows right away and adjust fine tuners while each individual plays. The first child whose instrument was tuned serves as the "A player" and follows the teacher around playing open A while the teacher tunes the rest of the class. If it is time for the lesson to begin, find someone else to quietly tune latecomers while getting the lesson started.

Check to see if the instruments are still in tune part-way through the lesson: play rhythms on open strings to individuals, and adjust fine tuners as they imitate those rhythms.

One basic group set-up is to have the students stand in rows (backs to the door) with the leader facing them to their left in front. (When the leader stands to the students' left, they are most likely to retain good "nose-bridge-elbow-toes" posture alignment as they

play.) For large groups the teacher may wish to put down lines of masking tape for the rows of students to stand on and a masking tape square for the leader to stand in. The students should be spaced far enough apart that one's outstretched left arm will barely touch the next one's right shoulder.

Some teachers move the students into appropriate rows; others let them organize themselves into rows within some time limit such as the playing of a "Twinkle" variation. Arrange taller students in the back and shorter students in the front. Taller students also fit in fairly well at the ends of rows. If there are only a few boys in a group, they can form a "boys' row" as long as there are no behavior problems. Any student with special needs should be placed right in front of the teacher. If the group is to meet on some repetitive basis, it saves future lesson time to have the students memorize their places and go straight to them at subsequent group meetings.

Place the piano to one side of the group so that the accompanist can see the teacher without craning his neck or growing eyes in the back of his head. If the piano is near the teacher, it will double as a convenient shelf for her instrument as needed. If accompanying a viola group, the piano accompanist needs to be capable of playing the melody as needed even though it may be written in alto clef only.

Begin the lesson on time to encourage punctuality. Many teachers begin and end each lesson with a respectful bow. The teacher bows to the class, and the class bows together to the teacher. Another beginning is simply starting a "Twinkle" variation; this gets everyone's attention.

After a basic warm-up exercise such as playing a few "Twinkles", the lesson begins. Keep everyone in the group actively involved as much as possible. Try to have direct eye, verbal, and touch contact with each student during the lesson. It should not be necessary to repeat instructions several times; try to *talk* less and *do* more.

## 1. Feet

Book One violin and viola students need constant review about rest position feet/ V-feet/ and playing position feet. They are playing their instruments now; when they concentrate on new things, they may lose good posture habits. To remind students of the importance of having their feet shoulder- width apart, *measure their shoulders* (with a bow or yard stick) and then check to see if their feet are that same distance apart.

Have the students take a little *jump* and see if their feet come down into good playing position again. This also aids in preventing locked knees. *Go on tiptoe* with them, saying, "Leave your ears up there while you put your heels back down." This helps the students to feel their spines lengthening and widening instead of compacting.

Have the students try to play a piece while *standing on one foot*. The left foot is the best to practice on, as most of the body weight should be on that foot anyway. When the weight is on the left foot, not only does the student play more "in" to his instrument, but he is also presenting himself in a confident way to the audience. If his weight is on his right foot, he has a "backing off" appearance.

## 2. Taking a Bow

Book One groups still need the bowing activities mentioned in the pre-Twinkle chapter of this book. Instruct the parents to applaud only if the group bows perfectly in unison. Have younger students bow as usual to a major chord; bow backwards to a minor chord; jump to staccato chords; and wiggle to arpeggiated chords. (The accompanist chooses which sort of signal to give at the end of each piece played.)

Try bowing in ways which tie in with what the students have just played. For example, bow with a smooth legato feeling after "Long, Long Ago". After "Song of the Wind", take a "staccato" bow: short and jerky. A deep, powerful bow symbolizes "forte"; a gentle bow approximates "piano".

## 3. Violin or Viola Hold

With their parents off to one side during the group lesson, students must become independent at setting their instruments on their shoulders correctly. Add a timing element to the activity *"On your mark, get set, GO!"*. In addition to the students' picking their instruments up from the floor and putting them into playing position as quickly as they can, (silently) count how many seconds it takes them to do it.

After checking to see that nose-bridge-elbow-toes are properly aligned, tap each child on the head saying, "You are a *statue*." They will quietly and patiently wait while a whole (small) group is turned into "statues". End the statue game in some way such as by having the statues play a piece or declaring them to be children again. A variation of this is to have the students *freeze* in the middle of playing a piece at some signal such as the teacher clapping her hands or calling out, "Freeze!" Then she checks everyone's postures. To check posture stability while playing, *wave or shake left hands* (with another student or a parent) during the open strings of a piece.

If sloppy postures are a problem, have the class play a piece together; if even one posture slips, everyone must *start the piece all over.* Do not specify exactly whose posture slipped.

### 4. Bow Hold

At least until late in Book One, violin and viola students use the *early bow hold.* (In the early bow hold, the student's thumb is placed on the clip of the bow outside the frog. This could be called an "outie" thumb!) Once their hand muscles are strong enough, they progress to using a *professional bow hold* by moving their thumbs to the stick, just above the frog. Now they have "innie" thumbs!

Continue the bow games outlined in the pre-Twinkle chapter of this book. *Tapping on right thumbs* reinforces the important bent-thumb concept. Have the students try to identify any mystery rhythms or pieces tapped on their thumbs: "taptaptaptap tap tap" is the first "Twinkle" variation.

While the class plays a piece together, watch their bow holds. If even one bow hold slips, everyone must *start the piece all over.* (Do not specify exactly whose bow hold slipped.)

**CONCENTRATION AND COORDINATION**

### 1. Hand and Feet Labels

Book One students need some occasional *drill* about which is the violin (or viola) hand and which is the bow hand. If the teacher is facing the group, some will become confused because their left is the teacher's right. The teacher may need to swing around so that her back is to the students and then raise her bow hand.

Build awareness that the bow thumb is bent, and the violin (or viola) thumb is relatively straight. The bow arm "sinks" while the other arm "floats". Playing "*ghost*" instruments is an excellent way to pinpoint any confusion: the students perform using imaginary instruments.

### 2. Memory Games

As a get-acquainted game as well as a memory game, have the students try to name every student in each row. (At an Institute, in addition to naming the student they should identify which city or state the student is from.) Then try this with eyes closed; can they remember in which order they are standing or what special things the others are wearing? Most challenging of all is trying to remember what each was wearing the last time the group met. The students should also learn the names of the accompanist and the group teacher. Check to see if the parents have been paying proper attention; can they name everyone in the group?

The *number sequence game, body parts*, and *memory of a pitch* activities as described in the pre-Twinkle chapter are excellent Book One activities. Practice thinking together through *counting out loud/counting silently*, in rhythm. If the teacher points to her mouth, the students count out loud. If she points to her ear, the students count silently (they think the numbers in their heads.) For example, the teacher points to her mouth and leads the class in counting "1-2-3" out loud. Then she points to her ear, signalling them to count 4-5-6-7-8-9 silently. She points to her mouth, and the class says, "10". This checks their developing pulse senses.

The counting game is easily expanded to *singing* and then to *playing instruments*. The students can alternate singing aloud/hearing the song in their heads or playing their instruments/hearing the piece in their heads. (Have a student signal turning the sound on or off by holding his bow vertically for "on" and horizontally for "off".) It is easier if the piano accompanist continues to play the music while the students hear their music in their heads. Eventually the accompanist as well as the students should be silent during the mental sections.

A planned variant of this is when the class plays a piece, deliberately *omitting a certain pitch*. For instance, the class plays "Twinkle" and rests whenever the E pitch is reached:

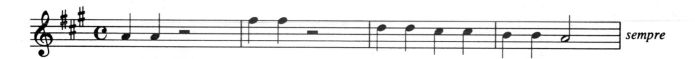

*sempre*

"The Happy Farmer" often triggers memory problems because of the two different endings to the opening, or "A", section. Play all of the piece very quickly (changing "The Happy Farmer" to "Super Farmer"!), except for the *troublesome endings*. Have the students supply the endings at the same fast tempo.

### 3. Identification Games

Book One students and their parents learn a lot about where they are headed through identification games. Play "*name that tune or rhythm*" (see the pre-Twinkle chapter); tailor the questions to each student.

Students of this level are ready to play the *snippets game*. They take turns performing a "snippet" (short section of the beginning, middle, or end of a piece) for the group. Those who think they know which piece the snippet is from raise their hands, and the performing student picks an answerer. If correct, the answerer gets to perform the next snippet. Instead of performing a snippet by playing his instrument as usual, a student could shadow bow or just clap the rhythm of a piece. Sometimes only one note is enough of a clue to guess the piece. (An up-bow E [A for violas] can only be the beginning of "O Come, Little Children" if the game is limited to the beginnings of Book One pieces.)

Book One students who have labelled the sections of "Twinkle" can *label the sections* of other pieces such as "Go Tell Aunt Rhody" (Bread/Baloney/Soft Baloney/Bread) or "Long, Long Ago" (Bread/Wheat Bread/Baloney/Soft Baloney/Wheat Bread). ("Soft Baloney" is an echo of the "Baloney" section.) Eventually the students learn the more conventional letter labels; for example, ABBA symbolizes the form of "Twinkle".

In addition to identifying *string names* as begun at pre-Twinkle groups, Book One students can begin to identify which *finger* the teacher plays on a given open string. As a first step, the teacher asks the class to identify whether she is playing the open string or using her first finger. She might later add second, and/or third fingers as variables. Some teachers use letter names right away. Their students identify "B" instead of "1 on A".

Book One students can also identify *out-of-tune notes*. The teacher plays, and the students raise their hands or pinch their noses if they hear an out-of-tune note. The teacher might play a Book One piece or just some third finger-open string octaves. An alternative is playing a passage twice and asking which time was correct.

Another hand game is to have the children clap or raise a hand whenever they *hear a certain pitch*, see a special bowing, etc., while the teacher performs a piece.

While more-advanced students play Suzuki's "Allegro", many teachers use some version of the following with early Book One students:

(Touch these body parts in quarter-note rhythm with hands)

Head    head/    Ears    ears/    Shoulders    shoulders/    Mouth    mouth/

Waist    waist/    Knees    knees/    Ankles    ankles/    Toes

Swing the arms in time during the contrasting section of "Allegro".

## 4. Concentrating Amid Difficulties

Do the students know their music so well that their playing becomes automatic, freeing them to concentrate on musicality? Some teachers have the students *converse* as they play. Others have them do whatever (silly) things the teacher does as they all play:

-stand on one foot
-turn around
-stick tongues out
-grin
-frown
-jump

Another way to test their growing ingrained habits is to have them concentrate amid difficulties at a group lesson. At some future point, today's Book One students will need the skill of concentrating on their own parts while surrounded by other parts. Have the students *play or sing different pieces* simultaneously. For example, some play a "Twinkle" variation while others play a different one. (The piano accompanist plays something non-commital such as simple chords.) A more difficult activity is for some to play the "Twinkle" theme while the rest play "May Song". (This also points up the similarities between those two pieces.) Most difficult is singing or playing a piece while others sing or play something completely different.

Have one or a few students try to play a piece while another tries to *distract* them. Tickling is not allowed, but the distracters may talk, sing, play different pieces, etc.

*Canons* also build concentration. In addition to singing a few well-known canons (or rounds) such as "Row, Row, Row Your Boat" or "Are You Sleeping", lead some canonic imitation. For example:

Teacher:  clap clap clap /snap snap snap /click click click
Class:                          clap clap clap   /snap snap snap

"Twinkle" Theme can also be done as a canon with the voices a measure apart.

In Variation B of "Twinkle", have the students clap or try to *touch their bow frogs to the tops of their heads* during each eighth-rest.

## 5. Focal Points

Some groups are drilled to focus on watching their bows according to Suzuki's maxim "eyes on bow". Other lessons train the students to focus on a leader, an important ensemble skill. An aid to emphasizing any focal point is the *eagle game*. Choose an individual or small group to be the "eagle(s)". The eagles can be parents or students; their job is to watch for group members who are slipping in their focal points and give them gentle taps on the tops of their heads. This game will make the children more aware of their focal points, but sometimes a student will not be capable of keeping that focus. It is negative to prolong the game while repeatedly tapping him on the head. Perhaps length of concentration may be built over several sessions.

Their ability to focus is much improved when the students *close their eyes* to play. When they close their eyelids, they open their "earlids".

## 6. Imitation

Play a simple sequence of open strings, fingers, rhythms, etc. and have an individual or group try to *duplicate the sequence*. This game is best played in rhythm. If necessary, say, "My turn-" and play the sequence in rhythm. Then say, "Your turn-" in rhythm before the class tries to duplicate the sequence.

Have the students *start when the teacher starts and stop when the teacher stops*. It helps for the teacher to lift her bow above the strings when she stops.

Play a version of the familiar children's game "Simon Says", changing the name to "*Suzuki Says*". The students only imitate the teacher if she first says "Suzuki says...".

### 7. Antiphony

"Antiphonal singing" is a term applied to singing in alternating choruses. It is applied here to students divided into subgroups stationed physically apart.

Divide the class into antiphonal groups (or individuals):
-each row performs only a specific section of a piece
-a small group in a corner (or an individual outside the room) performs an echo section alone
-certain groups perform only specific pitches of a piece (like a bell choir), or only the notes on a certain string
-different groups perform only until the teacher claps, signifying another group's turn
-two groups play different things and trade activities when the teacher claps (For example: some play "Perpetual Motion" singles while others play doubles; or some play "May Song" while others play "Twinkle" Theme)

### 8. Separate the Hands

A helpful practice activity is to *separate the hands.* The group pairs off, or each student uses a parent as a partner. One person bows while the other fingers the instrument. Those who bow should stand to the right of and slightly behind their partners.

### 9. New Twinkles

Invent *new "Twinkle" rhythms* for the students to try. By late in Book One, they may be able to handle a variation mixed with a triplet and a duplet:

They can also try *mixed versions* of the original variations:

***RIGHT HAND TECHNIQUES***

### 1. Basic Down and Up, With Articulations

Separating the functions of the right and left hands is an important practice tool. Have the students set their instruments on the floor and step back a pace. *Shadow bow* (bow up and down in the air with the bow held vertically) to introduce and reinforce proper bowings. While the students shadow bow a piece, check bow holds and point out retakes, hooks, and slurs. To shadow bow a comfortable distance from the body, have the students first reach "all the way out", then "all the way in", and finally "half-way out". Try to keep the bows going straight up and down.

Shadow bowing with proper *articulations* is an effective way to imprint the goal, even before learning a piece. Students and parents understand the difference between legato and staccato most clearly when they *experience it with their hands.* Hands rubbed smoothly together represent legato; hands rubbed with stops between each rubbing are like staccato. With pointed index fingers, a class can perform a Suzuki "Allegro" which resembles this drawing:

Then they can shadow bow the piece in a consistent place in the air. Do these activities while singing or humming the piece, to piano accompaniment, or while the teacher and other students play the

piece. The most difficult way to shadow bow is to bow together while everyone silently thinks the piece.

In addition to using proper bow articulation, Book One students can vary the lengths of bow they use. Use the amount of bow corresponding to the size of an ear, a nose, or a tooth.

## 2. Bow Arm

Book One students should continue the pre-Twinkle activity of bowing through *toilet paper rolls* held on their left shoulders. They can see their forearms open and close like a *door* while their upper arms stay relatively still. This provides another opportunity to check bow hold stability.

Book One students develop different *bow speeds* as they progress. Some teachers teach different bow speeds right away in "Twinkle" Variation A: the staccato eight notes equal the more legato sixteenth notes in bow length. "Lightly Row" and "Twinkle" theme are sung with "quick" for the quarter notes and "slow" for the half notes:

Quick quick slow,    quick quick slow,    *sempre*

Bow speeds get more sophisticated by "May Song". If the same bow speed is used for the dotted quarter notes and the eighth notes, a picture of lightening can be imagined while shadow bowing, bowing on an open string, or bowing in the piece:

At least by "Long, Long Ago" (if not in "Twinkle" Variation C), *bowing distribution* is an important concept to teach. Within a legato framework, the bow pattern for "Long, Long Ago" is: long short short/ long short short. The student should take a long down-bow on the first "long" note, placing the next "short" notes near the tip. On the next "long" note a long up-bow will place the following "short" notes near the frog. This may be more apparant to a group if demonstrated by rolling a small toy car down and up on a wall.

Book One students also experience *bow retakes*. (Some call these retakes bow lifts or bow circles.) The first time this occurs is in "Song of the Wind". Prepare a group for bow retakes by first isolating which direction the bow arm will move during a down-bow retake: counter-clockwise. The students pluck open strings with their right hands and then try "flying pizzicato": they take their hands away from their instruments in counter-clockwise circles after each pluck. Insist that the students set their right hands carefully before plucking; later it will be important to set the bow carefully for each retake. Try bow retakes on open strings and finally in the piece. Images such as making the bow circles the size of a watermelon, pickle, and peanut are helpful for building control. The students must *lift, set, and relax.* To drill a group on where the bow-retakes occur in a piece, have them turn around whenever they come to a retake. Once the students are farther along in Book One, they trade bows with partners during each bow retake in "Song of the Wind."

Have the students try to *silently lift and set* their bows on the string without letting their instruments "burp" (make inadvertent noises). Late Book One students can lift and set at the frog, in the middle, or at the tip. They can try rocking silently from string to string. Play "Twinkle" or "Perpetual Motion" with notes alternating being at the frog and the tip:

Book One students first play *bow accents* in "Allegretto". Their bow hands give their bows bursts of speed at the beginning of accented strokes. The following images may make the concept of an accent clearer to students:

  -push a rowboat into the water and then let it glide

  -watch fireworks explode and then shower down to earth

Once Book One students get to "Allegretto", they also need to try playing the previous pieces on the two middle strings (and the lower strings) instead of the upper strings as originally learned. (The piano accompanist must be prepared to play the pieces in new keys.) Some students may have a tendency to play on the middle strings with a suspended right upper arm. They will understand that this causes tension after they hold their elbows pointing up high in the air while the teacher plays a piece or sets a timer for a minute. They will be thankful to return to a relaxed, hanging feeling in their arms.

By "Minuet Two", violin and viola students begin to develop the ability to change from one string to another without necessarily using the entire bow arm. They may tip the bow from a higher to a lower open string *using just the bow hand.* Open "Minuet Two" with these lyrics:

El—bow, el—bow, hand and   whole   bow   arm

A way to isolate bow-arm technique is to play a piece without using the left- hand fingers. "Minuet Two" now begins:

If players play open D-open A repeatedly (starting down-bow on the D), their bow hands will make clock-wise circles.

Some teachers strictly train E- (or on viola, A-) string posture from the "Twinkle" varations; they have the bow arm initially set on E and then tip to A with the hand to start the piece. Other teachers have the students set the whole bow arm on A (D) and drop to E (A) when needed in the piece. The group teacher may see individuals who have been trained in different ways. The principles she should keep in mind and work for are the goals of *clean string crossings and firm tone.*

## 3. Tone

To demonstrate the *relaxed, hanging feeling* in a Suzuki bow arm, the teacher has students and parents make little shelves with their hands. She lays her relaxed bow arm onto each shelf. Most students and parents are surprised at how heavy a relaxed arm is. Explain that string players use this natural arm weight to bring a rich tone out of their instruments. Have the students and parents make shelves for each other and see how heavy their relaxed arms are. Check for relaxation, not pressure. If a bow arm is relaxed, it will flop when wiggled or if the shelf is pulled out from under it.

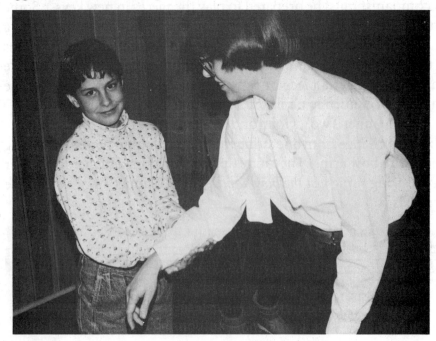

Book One violinists learn about the "*Kreisler Highway*". (Perhaps violists should label their bow path the "Primrose Highway"?) The students learn to have a consistent contact point where the bow hair and the string of the instrument meet. This contact point is generally between the upper end of the f-holes of the instrument and the bridge. Book One students gradually expand their bow usage in both directions from the middle of the bow. They may find it difficult to keep a consistent contact point while using longer bows later in the book. Practicing these tonal exercises on pieces such as "Long, Long Ago" is a good group activity. "*Eyes on bow*" is a fine exercise but may be physically difficult for those who wear glasses. "Eyes on bow" needs to progress to "*ears on bow*" anyway at some point; eventually the students will be watching a leader or written music instead of their own bows.

Have the students play a piece while holding their *bows upside-down*, at the tip instead of the frog. This gives a very weighted feeling which helps pull out a full tone. The students then turn their bows around again and immediately repeat the piece, trying to achieve that same full tone. Check each bow for proper weight on the string by *flicking the bow* lightly on the hair, above the contact point.

Have the students *feel the vibrations* of an instrument's scroll as someone plays open strings; this is similar to feeling the vibrations of a person's Adam's apple as he speaks. Students play lots of open strings in their early Suzuki pieces, as the open strings are the prototype of a big, ringing sound.

## LEFT HAND TECHNIQUES

### 1. Block, Prepared, or Independent Fingering

Teachers have differing opinions on when to introduce and use block, prepared, and independent fingering. (Block fingering means that two or three fingers go down on the instrument simultaneously, in a block. Prepared fingering occurs when the student is trained to first put down a finger and then put down another in relation to the first, such as 1 and then 2. Independent fingering happens when fingers are used only one a time.)

The group lesson is probably not the place to differ with individual techniques if they adhere to the basic principles of playing in tune with the fingertips and avoiding excess motion. If several students are "shooting" up their left fingers as soon as they have used them, have the students take turns holding their hands like *umbrellas* over the others' left hands as they play. This will discourage wasted left-finger "shooting" motion. Thinking of the left fingers "*walking*" around on the instrument strings while the hand is fairly stable also helps discourage wasted motion.

Straight left wrists make using fingertips easier, and some parents or students can be put on "*left-wrist patrol*" to help students keep their wrists from collapsing as they play. A solid instrument hold encourages a straight left wrist.

## 2. Finger Patterns

Until around "Etude", Book One students use only the finger pattern with a *high second finger*. Then the students learn to play with a *low second finger*. To combat the problem of out-of-tune second fingers, the teacher can perform a piece and stop before every second finger. An individual or the whole group then tells her whether to play "high 2" or "low 2". The students will hear if they are right or wrong.

The next new finger placement is *high third finger*. To practice this stretchy feeling, play "Hot Cross Buns" (easily learned by rote) starting on D#:

*Scales* are a good way to practice finger patterns. To play a scale in a round, have half of the group begin. Signal the others to begin when the first group is on the third pitch. To provide time to play together in tune, do a "Twinkle" rhythm on each pitch. Train the group to play the rhythm on the top note of the scale only once. Scales appropriate for students by the end of Book One are:

| *Violin* | *Viola* |
|---|---|
| One octave: A, D, G | One octave: D, G, C |
| Two octaves: G, A | Two octaves: C, D |

*MUSICALITY*

## 1. Dynamics

Try the "*Hot and Cold*" game. One student leaves the room, and another hides an object in the room. The first student returns, and the group helps him find the object by playing a pitch softly ("cold") when he is far from the object and loudly (" hot") when he is close, or vice versa.

One simple way of *signalling dynamics* is to have a leader open her hands wide for "forte" and clasp them together for "piano". A gradual widening of the distance between her hands signifies a crescendo; the closing of the gap is a decrescendo. Another simple way to signal dynamics is for the leader to hold her bow horizontally and move it high for "forte" and low for "piano". The rest of the group plays a piece while following these signals. The result is probably not particularly musical, but the students' awareness of dynamics grows tremendously. As a next step, signal dynamics more appropriate to the piece. Eventually the students should be able to tell what dynamic the teacher wants by watching the amount of bow she uses. The piano accompanist should exaggerate all dynamics.

## 2. Ensemble Skills

Book One students begin to develop ensemble skills. Try *starting pieces* in different ways:
- -with a piano introduction
- -with an introduction played by the teacher
- -with a rhythmically-stated "Ready-PLAY!"
- -with a breath

The students should learn to read the teacher's body language so that eventually they can start together after being signalled by a breath. The breath is with an imaginary preceeding beat. Let the students take turns being the leader and signalling with a breath. During "Allegretto", the students need to slow down together and then jump back into an "a tempo" section. They must follow the leader carefully to do so, keeping their eyes on the leader's bow.

*Watching the leader's bow* will also help to keep a group together in a piece such as "Perpetual Motion", where the constant eighth note pattern threatens to avalanche. In a small group, play "Perpetual Motion" or "Etude" with a metronome placed so that the students can watch its arm as they play. Playing together is more difficult if the piano accompanist drops out.

If there is no piano accompanist for the group, the teacher should play harmonies on her instrument or play the piece in a different octave than the students. The students will have better ensemble if they can hear the teacher, and they will hear her more easily if she is playing different pitches than they are. She should mirror the rhythms and bowings of the students' part as much as possible.

### 3. Exaggerate What Is Different

Students need to learn that what is clear to them is not always clear to an audience; they must *exaggerate* what is different. Difficult spots in pieces also need to be crystal clear. Take an individual or row at a time and check that each is playing the spot correctly. A saying in music goes: "a group is only as strong as its weakest player." One person playing incorrectly can spoil the careful work of the rest of the group.

Have the students "*serenade the audience*" by scattering around the room and playing to listeners. They return to their normal places for the end of the piece.

If the class performance was truly outstanding, a parent can signal this in some special way such as by *ringing a bell* provided by the teacher. An outstanding performance combines good posture, tone, intonation, bow technique, and clear musical ideas.

## COMBINED VIOLIN AND VIOLA GROUPS

Viola students really need separate groups to maintain their identity. Sometimes, however, it is necessary to combine them with violin students for a group lesson or performance. Putting purple ribbons on the viola scrolls helps the teacher to remember who plays what. Until fully grown, violists use the same instrument size they would use if they played violin; only the string placement is changed.

Once Book One violin students can play on their D strings, a combined group is fairly feasible. Some simple ways to adjust the Book One pieces for a combined group are:

- Violinists play 2-string pieces (through "Perpetual Motion") on D & A instead of on A & E. "Andantino", all of the Minuets, and "Happy Farmer" also work played one string lower than usual.
- Violists play "Lightly Row" in the key of A with the violins, using their 4th fingers for the E pitch.
- Violists play "Allegretto" starting on open D instead of open G.
- Violists play a simple harmony while the violinists play "Twinkle" in A:

Fine　　　　　D.C. al Fine

Violists can also play the melody of the middle section (Baloney) of "Twinkle" in the key of A if they use their fourth fingers for the E pitch. Have the violinists play the Bread sections and the violists the Baloney sections to make the whole "Twinkle" Sandwich.

Violists learn two pieces in Book One which violinists do not: "French Folk Song" and "Bohemian Folk Song". Have the violists perform these special pieces alone to show off their gorgeous "purple" tone, or teach the violinists these pieces so that the whole group can play them.

Technical exercises, concentration and coordination activities, and musical development are all appropriate for combined groups. When working on separating the hands, have the violists all bow and the violinists all finger or vice versa. Use this opportunity to play a piece that is not adjustable, such as "Etude" or the Gossec "Gavotte".

Viola students play the same-sized instruments as they would if they were violinists. The teacher should play on a real viola so that the students see that a full-sized viola is bigger than a full-sized violin and hear the rich viola tone.

## CENTRAL THEMES

The teacher may wish to organize the Book One lesson time with a central theme such as:

*Tone* (Model and work toward good tone.)

*Articulations* (Emphasize staccato and legato as found in the pieces.)

*Dynamics* (Focus on echoes in the early pieces; play forte or piano; add [de]crescendoes in the later pieces.)

*Ensemble* (Work at the class' ability to do everything together, from taking a bow to beginning and ending pieces.)

*Postures* (Keep returning to an emphasis on instrument and/or bow holds.)

*Five Senses* (Emphasize the ways in which we use our seeing, hearing, and sense of touch when we play our instruments.)

*Numbers* (Count how many times the students repeat activities, play the numbers memory game, check the sides of their squares, etc.)

*Copy Cats* (Feature a lot of imitation exercises; speak as little as possible.)

*Choosing Day* (Let the students or their parents choose which pieces to play, or have the students draw names of pieces out of a bag.)

*Concert Day* (Polish pieces for an upcoming group concert and run through them in concert order.)

## END OF LESSON

The final time of a Book One group may include activities where the students sit. They can listen to each other *play solos* and offer positive comments. Perhaps the teacher can perform a short piece for them. Students and parents learn that good concert manners involve listening quietly from a sitting position and applauding after a performance.

Another way to end a Book One group is to play the *"next piece" game.* The teacher begins to play a piece, and the students join in as soon as they can. After a few measures, the teacher lifts her bow and then launches into a different piece. The students re-join when they can; the accompanist will probably not try to keep up.

Place a small wrapped candy treat in each instrument's pegbox while the students play their final piece.

Use *crazy treats* to reward a hard-working group. Some ideas for crazy treats include:

-The students lie on the floor to play a piece.

-The students try to play their instruments using the wrong hands (right hand for the instrument, left hand for the bow).

-One student holds a bow steady vertically while another student holds an instrument horizontally, fingers it, and moves it up and down on the bow to play a piece. (Even a non-player can hold the bow.)

-The students play "Song of the Wind" at different speeds, building up from "Song of the Breeze" (slowly) to "Song of the Hurricane" (big, fast mess!).

-The parents perform "Twinkle" using their childrens' instruments.

Before putting away instruments and bows, many teachers like to end the class with a bow. The teacher bows to the students, and the students bow to the teacher.

# CHAPTER THREE:
## SUZUKI BOOK TWO

*INTRODUCTION*

Violin and viola students who are in Book Two have learned many basics of using the instrument and bow.

While tuning the students' instruments, instill an awareness of the tuning procedure as time permits. Perhaps the students can begin to adjust the fine tuners themselves; "righty-tighty and lefty-loosey" becomes a meaningful phrase. (To raise the string pitch, tighten the fine tuner by turning it to the right. To lower the string pitch, loosen the fine tuner by turning it to the left.) Students should either learn to use their left hands to adjust fine tuners or use their right hands while still holding their bows in their right hands. If they use their left hands to adjust the tuners, they will need to reach up to the tuners from under the bow, not via the left shoulder.

The "A 440" pitch is the only tuning pitch given to orchestra players. Students must learn to adjust their other strings in relation to the tuned A string. It helps them to hear the pitches of D, G, C, or E if they sing them. Sing "A" and a phrase on the same pitch such as, "This is an A. Please sing A with me". Give the students and parents a down-beat-like signal, and most will sing "A" as requested. Then play the A string of an instrument, sing on A something like, "This A is a little low. I'm going to tighten it up", and adjust it as needed. The students should be getting the concept of first listening to what is in tune and then listening to and adjusting what is questionable. Sing on the A pitch, "Now let's find the D." Sing:

Find the G pitch in a similar way. In a viola group, attempt the C pitch even though it is too low for most to sing. By singing part of the way down to it, the students will hear the rest of the notes including the C pitch more clearly in their heads. In a violin group, the students will need to remember the A pitch to be able to find the E pitch. Have them sing "A" again, and then help them sing:

Basic *warm-up exercises* include the "Twinkles" or a tonalization exercise. The teacher can plan the warm-ups to tie in with the group lesson emphasis of the day. For example, if she plans to use "dynamics" as the central lesson theme she might practice various dynamics in the warm-ups. If she plans to work on clear articulations, she demands clear articulations in the warm-up "Twinkles".

Many of the activities in this chapter can be used to preview pieces and techniques at the same time as more-advanced students play the pieces.

## POSTURE

### 1. Feet

Book Two violin and viola students still need occasional review about rest position feet/ V-feet/ and playing position feet. *Measure their shoulder widths* and then check to see if their playing position feet are that same distance apart. Many students are involved in sports activities and understand the need for a firm balance achieved by standing with feet shoulder-width apart.

Help the students become aware of how they *use their feet and whole bodies as they play.* Perhaps they tend to move with the bow (to the left with an up-bow; to the right with a down-bow). Perhaps they do the opposite. Some move their instruments only vertically, others horizontally. Build awareness of how individuals move and shift their balances. Encourage them to try moving in other ways. If feet are shoulder-width apart, knees are unlocked, and instruments are not rigidly cemented into shoulders, a variety of relaxed movement may be seen. When shifting balance, a player generally moves between left heel and right toes.

## 2. Violin or Viola Hold

Some Book Two students have lost their ability to keep their instruments up, parallel with the floor. Perhaps a student has a new instrument with an uncomfortable chinrest which needs replacing. Another student may have grown a lot recently and tends to droop all over. Once any instrument needs have been adjusted, combat the drooping instrument problem by having a shorter student or sibling *stand under the instrument scroll* of a taller student. The taller student tries to play a piece without letting the scroll hit the top of the other's head.

## 3. Bow Hold

By Book Two, most violin and viola students progress from using an early bow hold to using a *professional bow hold*. The bow games that were used to establish the early bow hold should be re-used for the professional hold. Check to see that students are not pressing with their first fingers in striving for a big sound; play a piece while holding the bow without using the first finger at all. Try playing without using second, third, or fourth bow fingers. The students can have a *spider race* by starting at the frogs and wriggling their bow hands to the tips and back down, with no help from left hands.

Firmly establishing bow holds at this level saves spending future time on remedial work. If even one bow hold slips while the class plays a piece, have everyone start the piece all over.

A tough bow-hold exercise is holding the bow at the tip and trying to *wriggle to the frog while playing "Twinkle"*, without losing good tone.

### 4. Relaxation Exercises

It is never too early to set the pattern of *instrument practice alternating with relaxation exercises.* Book Two students are probably too young and resilient to feel any pain when they play. However, if they develop poor playing habits and practice routines, they are likely to have physical aches and pains in the future.

Teachers try to instill good playing habits at individual lessons and help students find instruments, chinrests, and shoulder pads of proper size and comfort. This all contributes to relaxed playing. The group teacher can show the class some relaxation exercises to break up work sessions. After putting the instruments safely on the floor, some simple ideas for relaxation include:

-swinging both arms
-doing arm and shoulder circles of different sizes
-trying to clasp hands behind backs: one hand comes from over its shoulder, the other from under its shoulder
-twiddling the fingers and shaking the hands out
-wiggling
-rotating the neck and head

### 1. Memory Games

*CONCENTRATION AND COORDINATION*

The memory games as outlined in the Book One chapter of this book are also good standards for Book Two groups.

### 2. Identification Games

The "*name that tune or rhythm*" game first introduced at the pre-Twinkle stage is easily adapted for Book Two students. Check the ability to identify the three minuets from Book One and also the beginnings of: "Allegretto" and "Andantino"; and "Gavotte from 'Mignon'" and the Lully "Gavotte".

The "*snippets*" game as described in the Book One chapter is a good activity for Book Two groups.

Label the *basic sections* of "Waltz" and "Gavotte from 'Mignon'". Assign antiphonal groups different sections, and/or students who do not yet play the piece stand up or sit down to signify when the "A" section returns. "Gavotte from 'Mignon'" provides an opportunity to define the term *rondo form* as a piece where the beginning, or "A" section, returns sandwiched between other sections. "Gavotte from

'Mignon'" also has a *coda*, or "tail" section. Drill the different endings to the "A" sections of Waltz and Gavotte from 'Mignon'.

Book Two students have played many pieces in duple meter and some pieces in triple meter. They can identify which *pulse patterns* different pieces fall into. The accompanist or teacher performs a piece, and the students determine whether to feel the piece in groups of two or three (or four) pulses. The first pulse should be felt in a different way than the other(s); for example, the students tap their knees to the first pulse and clap to the other(s). Perhaps the students can count the pulse pattern out loud while playing an early piece. When defining "*syncopation*" (as in the Boccherini "Minuet"), have the students play "Twinkle" theme while the parents clap the off-beats.

As described in the Book One chapter, Book Two students should continue to identify string names and pitches. They can also identify common *musical terms:*

accompanist

arco

articulation (legato, staccato, spiccato)

composer (Bach, Bayly, Beethoven, Boccherini, Brahms, Gossec, Handel, Lully, Paganini, Schumann, Suzuki, Thomas, von Weber)

duet

dynamics (pianissimo, piano, mezzo-piano, mezzo-forte, forte, fortissimo)

ensemble

etude

harmonic

harmony

intonation

melody

metronome

pizzicato

rhythm

sequence

slur

solo

syncopation

tempo

trill

variation

Older Book Two students can try to spell these terms.

Book Two students can also begin to *identify intervals*. Begin by labelling the distances between notes as "intervals". Initially students

identify steps and skips. Gradually add other intervals:
    -perfect fifth (opening of "Twinkle")
    -perfect fourth (opening of "The Happy Farmer")
    -major third (opening of "May Song")
    -etc.

If this is an entirely new concept to most of the group, have the students in a particular row listen for only one type of interval and stand up if they hear "their" sound. Give the intervals in a variety of ways:
    -higher, then lower note
    -lower, then higher note
    -both notes played at once

If the Book Two students are preparing for music reading, have them call out note names while playing early pieces.

Hands learn to *react quickly* when a student and parent (or pair of students) hold their hands like this:

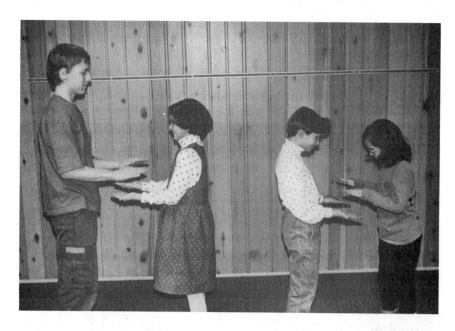

On a certain signal, the upper hands try to gently slap the lower hands while the lower hands try to escape. (Young children should always be the upper hands; some are too disappointed at being caught by the other person.) The best signal for this game is a wrong note played by the teacher. The more obvious the wrong note, the better.

*Clap and label simple rhythmic divisions.* Establish clapping a steady pulse, and label it "quarter notes". Then ask the class to clap "eighth notes", which are twice as fast. After returning to the quarter note pulse, try clapping "half notes" and then "whole notes".

## 3. Concentrating Amid Difficulties

The students should learn their music so well that their playing

becomes automatic, freeing them to concentrate on musicality. To check how ingrained playing the piece has become, have the students:
- converse as they play
- play or sing different pieces than others are playing or singing
- play a piece while someone tries to distract them
- play a piece much faster than usual ("Twinkle" becomes "Super Twinkle", or "The Happy Farmer" becomes "Super Farmer")

## 4. Focal Points

Playing the "*eagle game*" and having the students *close their eyes* when they play (see the Book One chapter) are also excellent Book Two activities. The students should be progressing from "eyes on bow" to "*ears on bow*". When they read music, they will be watching a conductor with their *peripheral* vision.

Exercise this vision through focussing on a point (straight ahead) and simultaneously watching and following the leader.

Have the students stand in *back-to-back lines*. While each student plays, he listens to the player behind him. If he hears the player behind him make a mistake, he bops him with his behind!

## 5. Imitation

This game (as outlined in the Book One chapter) is adaptable to any level: a leader plays a simple sequence of open strings, fingers, rhythms, etc., and the students try to duplicate it. The teacher may wish to add the pressure that anyone who errs must sit down.

## 6. Antiphony

Antiphonal groups as described in the Book One chapter are appropriate for the Book Two level.

## 7. Old Pieces in New Keys

Book Two students learn a variety of finger patterns and can exercise them through trying earlier pieces in new keys. (The piano accompanist may need a little warning about this.) Give the Bb (Eb for violas) scale finger pattern a workout by playing the first section of "Perpetual Motion" beginning on Bb instead of A (Eb instead of D for violas). To work on low second fingers, play any early Book One piece in the next key down (G instead of A for violins, C instead of D for violas). To work on the high third finger, play "Twinkle" one whole step higher than usual.

## 8. Passage Work

When working on a difficult spot, build the passage adding only one new note at a time. (The teacher cues the students' turn with her bow or a nod of her head):

First time - teacher only.  Repeat - teacher and group or group only.

### 9. Extra-Challenging Twinkles

In addition to "Twinkle" Variations AB and CD (see the Book One chapter), try "Twinkle" ABCD:

An easier variation of "Twinkle" ABCD is to play the Variation A rhythm in the first section of "Twinkle", Variation B in the second section, Variation C in the third section, and Variation D in the fourth section.

Another challenging "Twinkle" activity is for the class imitate any *bowing mistakes* the teacher makes while they all play.

*RIGHT HAND*
*TECHNIQUES*

### 1. Basic Down and Up, With Articulations

Separating the functions of the right and left hands is an important practice tool for players of all levels. *Shadow bowing* (bowing down and up vertically in the air) is described in the Book One chapter of this book. It is still useful at a Book Two group lesson.

To reinforce where *slurs* occur in a piece, choose a two-syllable name to say at each two-note slur, as in the following excerpt from "Musette":

Nora, Nora,  Nora  Nora  Nora  Nora Meyer

### 2. Bow Arm

Book Two students gain a lot of bow arm technique through playing the Suzuki pieces, including the development of different *bow speeds.* Have a slow bow contest: the students start playing a note at the frog of the bow and see which person can take the longest to get to the tip of the bow while still producing a sound. To practice different bow speeds at a group lesson, play a scale or the basic tonalization exercise, going from *pianissimo to forte* on each note (slow bow to fast bow) or vice versa.

In some Suzuki pieces such as "Musette", there are spots with "*MORE-less" slurs*: use more bow (thus, faster speed) on the first note and less (slower) bow on the second:

"MORE-less" slurs should be practiced both up-bow and down-bow. The Beethoven "Minuet" has several notes under a slur, and some of the notes are accented. This entails a whole string of "MORE-less" slurs:

Another exercise for working on bow speeds under a slur is to play the basic tonalization exercise with surges of bow speed on each note:

When reviewing Book One pieces such as "Minuet 1", add the skill of using a *slower bow at phrase endings.* Use gradually *more (or deeper) bows during crescendoes* and the opposite during decrescendoes. A good spot to work on this occurs in the Handel "Bourree":

53

Book Two students also gain *control of the entire bow.* Try playing exercises or pieces at the frog, then in the middle, and finally at the tip of the bow. The teacher checks to see that the tip of the bow, the right hand, and the right elbow all move together. To make this more difficult, hold the bow in the middle of the stick and play at the tip and then at the frog.

Have a *whole bow contest,* all trying to play a piece (such as "Chorus") using whole bows. Those who do not use the whole bow, frog to tip, must sit down. (Each row of students is judged by a parent, who taps those using less than whole bows.) Make the contest increasingly difficult by speeding up the tempo of the piece each time it is replayed.

Work to *control the strength of both up-bows and down-bows.* When playing a piece with constant equal rhythms (such as "Etude" or "Perpetual Motion"), have the audience listen with eyes closed. The listeners should be unable to tell whether the players started down-bow or up-bow; all the strokes should sound equally strong.

Book Two students can also experience some *off-the-string bowings.* Show the students how to find the balance points of their bows: balance the bows on outstretched left index fingers. Mark this spot with a little piece of tape if necessary. Play "Perpetual Motion" with repeated down-bow circles near the balance point. Then try doing all of the notes up-bow. Finally try the piece with scooped, off-the-string bows: one note down-bow, the next note up-bow. Try for a brushed stroke similar to sweeping with a wisk broom; all the strokes should sound equally strong. Try lifting off the string at the ends of up bows in places in "Hunter's Chorus" and the "Long, Long Ago" variation:

Suzuki pieces such as the "Long, Long Ago" variation and the trio section of the Beethoven "Minuet" demand *repeated up-bow staccato strokes.* Try "Twinkle" Variation D or "Perpetual Motion" with 2, 4, 8, or 16 notes per bow:

The right thumb gives a little power thrust to each note in repeated same-bow staccato. It also gives a burst of speed to the bow in *accents*, first practiced in Book One. The up-beat accented notes in "Witches' Dance" help make the phrasing clear:

Have the audience clap with the accented notes in "Witches' Dance". The syncopated rhythms in the Boccherini "Minuet" are very exciting when performed with clear accents. Practice *quick accents* in "Twinkle" Variation D, "Perpetual Motion", or "Etude". Accent only the initial note of each group of four notes. (Have the parents clap with each accented note.) Next accent only the second note of the group; then the third; and finally the fourth.

The right thumb also helps *give the bow a burst of speed during trills*, which are introduced in Book Two. "Sting" the trill; give a burst of speed to both hands at the beginning of a trill.

Book Two pieces are increasingly challenging in terms of *string crossings*. Drill difficult spots by stopping the bow prior to the string crossing or under the slur. Gradually speed up the exercise until the class can perform the spot at the proper speed. For example, break the first measure of "Waltz" into the following exercises:

First time - teacher only
Repeat - teacher + group or group only

### 3. Pizzicato

Students must pluck their instruments in the Gossec "Gavotte". In that particular spot they maintain a basic bow hold and reach out with their first fingers to pluck, "as though they were going to scratch their noses". Pizzicato again occurs at the end of "Gavotte from 'Mignon'". In this particular spot there is time to switch to grabbing the bow, freeing up the thumb to anchor the right hand while the first finger plucks. Practice changing from a playing bow hold to a plucking bow hold.

Have the class play an entire piece pizzicato.

### 4. Tone

Book Two students work for a good, firm sound on all four strings using each section of the bow. If they trade instruments at a group lesson, they will discover that each instrument has its own individual best *contact point* for maximum sound. Experiment with sliding the bow across a string from the fingerboard toward the bridge until the instrument suddenly rings out with a better sound. Initially this contact point is controlled through watching it, but "eyes on bow" needs to progress to "*ears on bow*" at some point. Have the students close their eyes to play. As described in the Book One chapter, using *natural arm weight to pull out a strong tone* is a central element of the developing bow arm.

Have the parents turn their backs to the students, who each take turns playing the tonalization exercise. Each parent *raises his hand if he recognizes his child's playing.*

Violists' tone is often described as a deep "*purple*". Wearing purple clothes helps keep this in mind. *Red* is also a strong color; if the teacher wears something deeply red, the students will have a visual example of the tone to pull out of their instruments.

*LEFT HAND TECHNIQUES*

### 1. Independent Fingering

If vibrato exercises are to be started by the late Book Two stage, students must be using independent fingering by then. This is useful to point out and define at group lessons.

Using a straight left wrist is also important for future vibrato development. As suggested in the Book One chapter, set up a "*left-*

*wrist patrol*" to help students keep their wrists from collapsing as they play. A solid instrument hold makes the wrist less likely to collapse.

Check for intonation security by having the students play a note, drop their left hands to their sides, and then replay the note. The pianist, the teacher, or a student holds out the note so that everyone has the correct pitch in mind. This is a good exercise to check individually in a small group.

## 2. Finger Patterns

In the "Concentration and Coordination" section of this chapter, playing *familiar pieces in new keys* is suggested for practicing concentration as well as new finger patterns. Scales are also a good way to practice finger patterns. By the end of Book Two, students can play the following scales:

| Violin | Viola |
|---|---|
| One octave: C, D, E, F | One octave: F, G, A, Bb |
| Two octaves: G, A, Bb | Two octaves: C, D, Eb |

Students should be using their *fourth fingers* quite often by this time. A simple fourth finger exercise is to have the group play "Lightly Row" all on one string.

*Good finger posture* is encouraged by playing pieces such as "Go Tell Aunt Rhody" or "Long, Long Ago" with adding simultaneous open E's (A's for violas).

Another exercise is to play "Go Tell Aunt Rhody" as usual while holding the fourth finger down on the D string (G for violas). Yet another exercise is to play "Perpetual Motion" alternating each note of the piece with fourth finger.

To practice the augmented second found in the Lully "Gavotte", try "Aunt Rhody Goes to Arabia":

### 3. Intonation

Book Two students are at least in the process of being weaned from their fingerboard tapes. Their ability to hear when they play in tune is growing. They can also *feel* when they play certain notes in tune; notes which make open strings ring in sympathetic vibration give fingers a tickly feeling when accurate, and students can see the string vibrating. How long and well individual instruments keep *ringing* is interesting to discover at group lessons.

### 4. Ornaments

The first Suzuki piece to use a grace note is the Gossec "Gavotte". Some play that grace note before the beat; others play it on the beat. As long as the group teacher has a group all do the grace note one way or the other, the performance of the piece will not suffer. This is an example of two different yet both acceptable musical ideas.

The two grace notes in "Waltz" are difficult for students to execute quickly enough and with the correct bowing. Work on this problem through the following exercise:

Think of the third finger as touching something hot on the fingerboard and quickly coming up again.

A trill-like figure is present in "Gavotte from 'Mignon'", and true trills occur in the Lully "Gavotte" and the Boccherini "Minuet". To practice trills, have the group play "Twinkle" with 3- and 5-note trills:

(3 - note trills)　　　　　　　　　　　　　　　　　　　(5 - note trills)

### 5. Shifting

Shifting is necessary for viola students in the Lully "Gavotte" and the Beethoven "Minuet". Violin students can benefit from some shifting exercises by late in Book Two also.

Teach shifting *without instruments* initially. Have the students play imaginary instruments and shift to and from low and high positions.

Point out that their left thumbs and elbows *move* while their hands shift high and low. Then the students try this sort of exercise on their instruments. The teacher turns her back to the students so that they can see her left thumb moving more under the instrument's neck as her hand shifts up. Swoop up to a high position, reach over with left fingertips, and tap to the left of the fingerboard. Check to see that left thumbs and elbows are not left behind during shifting.

The students experience gradually using higher positions when playing the first phrase of "Perpetual Motion" in progressively higher keys:

To practice jumping between first and third position, teach the group the *Target Shifting Song* by rote:

(This piece was written by Suzuki cello teacher Carey Beth Hockett, who calls it "Countdown". It is used here with her permission.) The name "Target Shifting Song" teaches the idea that in shifting practice a player does not re-adjust missed notes any more than an archer runs out to a target and re-adjusts his arrows. When a group plays the "Target Shifting Song", any students not yet ready to shift can play the piece entirely in first position. Play the piece on any pair of strings.

## 6. Natural Harmonics

Viola players use a natural harmonic at the end of "Musette" and in the Beethoven "Minuet". Violin as well as viola players often put a natural harmonic into the Trio section of the Boccherini "Minuet" during the last accompaniment figure in the solo part:

Practice natural harmonics in this version of the "Target Shifting Song":

## 7. Vibrato

Though few Book Two students achieve vibrato control, many are ready for pre-vibrato exercises. This may boost their awareness of and desire to learn vibrato.

One simple analogy for teaching vibrato is to demonstrate how a baby learns to *wave*. First a baby waves bye-bye with her whole arm. Then she learns to wave with her hand and wrist. When she grows up and becomes a teenager, she waves with just her fingers! Early vibrato exercises involve the whole arm. Gradually the students progress to exercises involving the hand and wrist, and finally they will build vibrating skills in their fingers.

Another simple vibrato analogy is for the teacher and students to pretend that their bodies are *giant finger joints* with their real feet representing the fingertips on the strings. Sway from side-to-side to simulate the direction the finger rocks on the string. Sway back and forth, in circles, or hop up and down to demonstrate incorrect vibrato motions.

Have the students wave at themselves with their left hands. Wave at *different speeds*: fast and slow. Wave from slightly to the right of their playing-position instruments; then gradually wave from closer to the instruments' necks. Finally, wave from first position. Then put a finger down on a middle string and *slide it up and down* the string in approximately whole steps. Swoop up to a high position (similar to an early shifting exercise), and slide the finger up and down the string in approximately whole steps again. Swoop down to a low position and repeat the exercise. This exercise can also be done with a piece of kleenex placed under a finger between the middle strings to *polish* the fingerboard.

Have the students practice vibrato on their own right *forearms*; pretend that the forearm is an instrument neck. (Squeezing the instrument neck is a common vibrato problem, but people do not tend to squeeze their own arms.) First the students slide their whole left hands from right wrist to elbow, and gradually they decrease how far they slide. Put one left finger on the topside of the right forearm and rock it back and forth, from wrist-direction to elbow-direction. Try this with the left thumb touching or not touching the underside of the right forearm. Try vibrating on right palms.

Demonstrate a beautiful vibrato in a familiar piece so that the students see and hear what they will strive for when they are more advanced. Caution them not to try using vibrato until their private teacher says that they are ready.

*MUSICALITY*　　## 1. Ensemble Dynamics

To demonstrate the necessity for dynamics in music, tell the class a *short story*. Use a monotone voice with no dynamic relief. In the same voice, ask what to do to make the story more interesting. Begin the story again and again with their suggestions added. Sooner or later a student will ask in some way for dynamics.

Ensemble skills as outlined in the Book One chapter apply to Book Two groups also. Control *dynamic changes* together in "Twinkle":

*Fine*　　**f - p**　　*D. C. al Fine*

When students play together with their *eyes closed*, their ears become more attuned to what the others around them are doing.

In addition to having a student signal when to turn the sound on and off in a piece, add another level of difficulty by having a second student signal what dynamic to play. (The on/off signal is a bow turned vertically/horizontally. The dynamics are signalled with hands far apart for forte and close together for piano.)

## 2. Awareness Of What Is Fitting Together

Students play an *accompanying* figure in the trio of the Boccherini "Minuet". Ask if anyone can sing what the piano plays while the violin or viola plays this accompaniment figure. The students should be building awareness of what is fitting together with their music to make up the whole work. Can they name some pieces in which the piano plays a "boom-chick" part? ("Allegretto", "Andantino".) In which piece does the piano have the melody in the left hand instead of the usual right hand? ("The Happy Farmer".)

### 3. Silence

Book Two students can begin to be aware of the importance of *silence* in music. At the beginning of "The Two Grenadiers", the violin or viola player sometimes has a half-note followed by a rest, and sometimes has a dotted half-note:

The rhythmic pulse of the piece is not damaged when someone plays through the rest, but part of developing musicianship is learning to be precise. In the trio section of the Boccherini "Minuet", the soloist's rests are quite important during the accompaniment figure. If the soloist skips the rests, the accompanist must squash the melody and pulse. Towards the end of "Gavotte from 'Mignon'", the violin or viola part has a full measure of rest. Anyone who has "fallen into" this rest during a group lesson knows how embarrassing that can be; the silence is a very exposed part of the piece.

## 4. Dances

Book Two students perform many pieces originally written as *dances.* Some are in duple meter (gavottes, bourrees) while others are in triple meter (minuets, waltzes). Gavottes often begin with "tip-toe" notes:

### 5. Exaggerate What Is Different

Students learn to exaggerate what is different when they play. Bow articulations, dynamics, rhythmic changes, phrases, tempi... all need to be crystal clear to an audience. Practice *versatility* through exercises such as beginning a piece in any tempo which the teacher signals with a breath.

The students can *serenade the audience* by scattering and playing to individuals and returning to their normal spots by the end of the piece.

Keep working at a piece until the performance rates the ringing of a special *bell* by a listening parent.

*COMBINED VIOLIN AND VIOLA GROUPS*

Viola students really need separate groups to maintain their identity. Sometimes, however, they must be combined with violin students. In addition to the ideas presented for this situation at the end of the Book One chapter, Book Two pieces can be adjusted in the following ways for a combined lesson or performance:

-violinists start a string lower on 3-string pieces:

"Chorus" "Waltz" "Two Grenadiers"

"Musette" "Bourree" "Witches' Dance"

-violists play "Long, Long Ago" and its variation starting on the D string if they use their fourth fingers on A for the E pitch

-violists play "Twinkle" in the key of A with the violins by shifting to third position when necessary:

"Hunters' Chorus" and the Beethoven "Minuet" are in the same key for both violinists and violists.

*CENTRAL THEMES*

In addition to central themes listed at the end of the Book One chapter, the teacher may wish to organize a Book Two lesson with a central theme such as:

*Bowing Distribution*

*Ornaments* (Feature grace notes and trills.)

*Old Pieces New Ways* (Play pieces in new keys and positions.)

*Marathon Review Day* (Play all the pieces from Book One and/or Two.)

*Birthday Day* (Feature a composer: play pieces by that composer; show a portrait of him; etc. See the end of this book for a listing of composers' birthdays)

**END
OF
LESSON**

At the end of a Book Two lesson, the students can listen to or play *solos*, play the *"Next Piece Game"* (described in the Book One chapter), or do some crazy treats. New *crazy treat* suggestions are:

-Hold instruments behind backs and pluck a song using the right hand

-Perform the "Witches' Dance" dance (see page 66)

-Play "Twinkle" with a bow twirl during each half-note (hold the bow in the middle of the stick and turn it half-way around)

-Stand in a line (tallest to smallest); each bows his neighbor's instrument

-Point scrolls at different walls of the room whenever certain pitches occur in a slowly-played early piece. (For example: A=north wall; B=south wall; etc.)

# "Witches' Dance" Dance

# "Witches' Dance" Dance

# CHAPTER FOUR:
## SUZUKI BOOK THREE

*INTRODUCTION*　　　Book Three violin and viola students have learned many basics of using the instrument and bow and begin to do at least some elementary shifting and vibrato exercises.

Basic *warm-up* exercises include the "Twinkles" or a tonalization exercise. The teacher can plan the warm-ups to tie in with the group lesson emphasis of the day. Try Suzuki's basic tonalization exercise with the following variations:

-start up-bow instead of down-bow (make each note sound equally strong)

-use whole bows, half bows, or some other pre-determined amount

-use the rhythm of a quarter note and four sixteenth notes on each pitch to practice smooth exchanges from down-bow to up-bow

-do a crescendo, decrescendo, or "hairpin" (cresc./decresc.) on each pitch

-use different contact points: "Kreisler highway"; sul tasto; ponticello

-compare each G, D, A, or E (C, G, D, or A for violas) with open strings-

　　A. Teacher plucks these open strings as students play

　　B. Students pluck these open strings as others play

　　C. Students play tonalization but stop and check each note that matches an open string

*POSTURE*　　　All of the posture activities outlined in the Book Two chapter are pertinent to Book Three students:

-awareness of feet and whole bodies

-instrument hold

-bow hold

-relaxation exercises

*CONCENTRATION*
*AND*
*COORDINATION*

### 1. Memory Games

Some of the memory games suggested in the Book One chapter of this book are suitable for Book Three groups:

-remembering names, states, order in which standing, clothes worn

-developing pitch memory

-checking troublesome endings (Common Book Three culprits are the "C" and "C1" sections of the Martini "Gavotte"; the endings to the "A" section of "Humoresque"; the "A" and "A1" sections of the Becker "Gavotte".)

## 2. Identification Games

The *"name that tune"* game first introduced at the pre-Twinkle stage is easily adaptable for Book Three level students.

Label the *basic sections* of the gavottes and "Humoresque" in Book Three. Assign antiphonal groups to different sections. Have students who do not yet play the piece stand up or sit down when they hear a certain section.

Continue to identify which *pulse patterns* different pieces fall into, as described in the Book Two chapter. The students can even try *conducting* simple patterns.

Reinforce common *musical terms.*

Continue to build on the ability to *identify intervals.* Students seldom have a preconceived notion that this is a difficult thing to do, though their parents may.

To make the quick-reaction *hand-slapping game* more difficult, have the signal be an out-of-tune note instead of a completely wrong pitch. Partners can alternate having their hands be the slappers or the slappees. Most difficult of all is to have each partner try one hand being a slapper and the other hand being a slappee. It must be emphasized that this is a gentle game, meant only in fun. If the learning situation deteriorates, go on to something else immediately.

Continue to *clap and label simple rhythmic divisions.* This is more challenging if the students are divided into groups which clap different rhythms simultaneously.

## 3. Concentrating Amid Difficulties

A concentration test for Book Three groups is to have some of the class play Bach's "Minuet No. 3" while others play the minor section added in Book Three. The two sections of the piece will not harmonize, but the students will see that the minor section is quite similar to the original minuet and will get a good concentration work-out. Those who enjoy this activity may wish to listen to some of the music of Charles Ives.

## 4. Focal Points

Book Three students need to control their bow contact points with their ears, by listening for a consistent sound. At the same time, test their ability to watch a leader out of the corners of their eyes with their peripheral vision.

## 5. Imitation

The imitation game as outlined in the Book One chapter is adaptable to the Book Three level: the leader plays a simple sequence of open strings, fingers, rhythms, etc., and the group tries to duplicate it.

### 6. Antiphony

Antiphonal groups as described in earlier chapters are still appropriate for Book Three groups.

### 7. Old Pieces in New Keys

Book Three students have experienced many left-hand finger patterns and can exercise them through trying earlier pieces in new keys. (The piano accompanist may need a little forewarning.) Try changing a piece (such as "Bohemian Folk Song") from minor to major:

*etc.*

### 8. Passage Work

The idea of building a difficult passage adding only one new note at a time is in the Book Two chapter. Additional ways to practice difficult spots at group lessons include *hiccups* and *doubles*, as in this excerpt from the minor section of the Bach "Menuetto":

An entire group's performance of a difficult passage will sound muddy if only one or two are careless. Have each student *play the difficult spot alone.* This usually provides the incentive to work a little harder.

Difficult spots need a lot of simple *repetition.* Ask the class if they know how many times Dr. Suzuki asks his students to repeat things: ten thousand times! Tens or hundreds of repetitions seem attainable compared to ten thousand.

## *RIGHT HAND TECHNIQUES*

### 1. Basic Down and Up, With Articulations

Separating the functions of the right and left hands is an important practice tool for players of all levels. Introduce and reinforce pieces with *shadow bowing* (described in the Book One chapter).

## 2. Bow Arm

Control of different *bow speeds* is central to Book Three students' expressive playing. Many of the pieces have spots with "*MORE-less*" slurs slightly more complicated than those present in Book Two. In this spot in "Gavotte in g minor" the Bb is the "MORE" and the A is the "less". The following G is another "less":

In "Gavotte in D" ("Gavotte from Orchestral Suite" to violists), the up-bow "MORE-less" in the following spot occurs after a slightly-stopped down-bow:

Book Three students continue to develop the skill of using a *slower bow at phrase endings*. They also use gradually *deeper bows during crescendoes* and the opposite during decrescendoes. In "Gavotte in g minor" the opening crescendo occurs under a slur and can be practiced the following way:

Awareness of bow speeds aids in planning for *bow distribution*. A piece such as "Humoresque" has some "tip traps" to avoid:

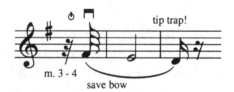

Book Three students need *control of the entire bow*. As described in the Book Two chapter, try playing pieces at the frog, middle, or tip of the bow. Check to see that the tip of the bow, the right hand, and the right elbow all move together.

Book Three students also continue to *control the strength of both up-bows and down-bows*. Not only should they be capable of making both bow directions sound equally strong, but they should develop awareness of changing the strengths of certain notes to fit the musical line. In the B section of the Becker "Gavotte" the three repeated D's need to build in strength regardless of bow direction:

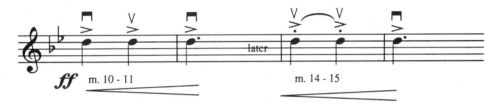

The right thumb continues to *give the bow a burst of speed during trills*. The trills in "Gavotte in D" ("Gavotte from Orchestral Suite") should make listeners almost jump in their seats!

*String crossings* are presented with increasing difficulty in Book Three. In the Bach "Bourree", rapid crossings are sometimes combined with chords. Drill difficult spots by stopping the bows prior to the string crossing or under the slur. Gradually speed up the exercise until the class can perform the spot at the proper tempo.

### 3. Tone

Book Three students strive for a good, firm sound on all four strings using each section of the bow. They try to control their *contact points* (where the bow hair meets the instrument string) and use *natural arm weight* to pull out a strong tone. Students are helped by thinking of the bow hair wrapping around the string, which can be "magnified" and shown by the teacher wrapping her right fingers around her outstretched left index finger.

Students try to maintain a solid sound while using different dynamics. A "piano" sound does not have to be wispy, and a "forte" sound does not have to be crunchy.

The introduction to this chapter contains ideas for working on tone production in Suzuki's "tonalization" exercise.

**LEFT HAND TECHNIQUES**

### 1. Fingers

Occasionally students need to put a finger down on *two strings at once*. An example occurs near the end of the minor section of the Bach "Minuet" in Book Three:

m. 75

Continue to practice finger patterns by playing familiar pieces in *new keys and scales*.

The g-minor pattern (c-minor for violas) is often difficult for string players to keep in tune. The first finger (Bb for violins, Eb for violas) must be played low (next to the nut of the instrument), and yet the third finger should not be allowed to pull flat. This interval will feel stretchy to the left hand. An exercise for this feeling is:

## 2. Ornaments

Playing "Twinkle" with 3- and 5-note trills was described in the Book Two chapter and is still a good exercise for Book Three students. Try starting the trill from the upper note:

The Bach "Gavotte in D Major" ("Gavotte from Orchestral Suite") provides an opportunity to demonstrate two different yet both acceptable musical ideas. Some teachers teach the grace note before the beat, while others teach it on the beat but very quick, almost an appoggiatura.

Spots with ornaments should be practiced without the ornaments. This can be called playing the "tree". Some of the students play the "tree" while the rest play the "tree with ornaments"; check that tempo is not lost during the ornament.

## 3. Pizzicato

No new pizzicato passages occur in Book Three, but the students should continue to practice plucking now and then. Pluck open strings with left fingers as a strengthening exercise.

## 4. Shifting

Viola students have to shift several times in Book Three pieces. Violin students do shifting exercises in preparation for Book Four. Early shifting exercises are in the Book Two chapter of this book. Book Three students can also try an early piece such as "Twinkle" in a different position, usually third position.

A more-difficult version of the "Target Shifting Song" which may be learned by late Book Three involves first, second, and third positions:

Students learn to listen carefully when they *keep score* of in-tune notes while someone plays the "Target Shifting Song". The G is played five times, and each time it is in tune the scorer holds up one finger. Use the other hand to mark achieving the five D's in tune. Getting "Perfect Fives" is a real challenge.

## 5. Vibrato

Early vibrato exercises are in the Book Two chapter. Another exercise appropriate for Book Three students is to vibrate in *rest position*. Just as the students did on their forearms, they now slide their left hands from the nut to the shoulder of the instrument. Gradually decrease the length of the slide. Put one finger on a middle string and rock it back and forth, nut-direction to shoulder-direction. Try this with left thumbs touching or not touching the instrument necks.

Finally, the students try to vibrate in *playing position*. They still do not use their bows to hear how this sounds; too many will inadvertently try to vibrate with their bow hands! After warming up with sliding left hands back and forth from the nut to the shoulder of the instrument, decrease the distance of the slide. Put one finger on a middle string and rock it back and forth. If necessary, another person gently holds the student's left forearm to discourage excessive arm motion.

Always vibrate when playing with the class so that the students have a good visual image of vibrato.

### 6. Double Stops

Book Three students play some double stops at the end of the book. To prepare for the double stops in "Gavotte in D Major" ("Gavotte from Orchestral Suite" for violists), have the class play "Double Twinkle", adding the next open string at all times:

*sempre*

*MUSICALITY*

As presented in the Book Two chapter, dynamics, ensemble skills, and awareness of what is fitting together to make the whole piece are central elements of helping students play musically.

### 1. Exaggerate What Is Different

Musicians exaggerate what is different. In Book Three the prevailing key is g-minor (c-minor for violas). If the Bb (Eb) is not played low enough, that one note will change the feeling of the key of the piece to major. Bow articulations, dynamics, rhythmic changes, and phrasing all need to be exaggerated to come across to the audience. Use *eyebrows* to highlight the need for exaggeration; signal playing a note higher or louder with raised eyebrows.

### 2. Phrases

Book Three students experience different sorts of phrases. "Gavotte in g minor" opens with an *arch-shaped melody* which should be brought out by dynamics:

"Humoresque" also opens with a basically arched-shaped melody. The "B" section of "Humoresque" is quite a contrast to this; it has a wide leap in its melody.

Another sort of phrase is found in the "*question-answer*" opening of "Gavotte in D Major" ("Gavotte from Orchestral Suite"):

### 3. Direction of Line

Book Three students continue to learn to give direction to their sequences. Bring out the *moving line* in the Bach "Bourree":

m. 5

### 4. Registers

Book Three students have gained control of different registers of their instruments. The "C" section of "Humoresque" has a much deeper, lower sound than the "B" section which came before it. If played in third position, the "C" section has an even richer timbre:

m. 33

### 5. Characters

The different registers in "Humoresque" compliment contrasting *musical characters* in the sections. Some teachers call the three sections "teams": good guys; ladies; and bad guys. Others use analogies such as butterflies, birds, and bears.

Book Three students can experience the joy of performing a piece well and with individual musical expression.

**COMBINED VIOLIN AND VIOLA GROUPS**

Viola students need separate groups to maintain their identity but sometimes must be combined in a group with violin students. In addition to the ideas provided for this situation at the ends of earlier chapters, have violinists play 3-string pieces starting a string lower:

Martini "Gavotte" (except for 1 note)
"Minuet"
"Gavotte from Orchestral Suite"

"Gavotte in g minor" and the Becker "Gavotte" are in the same key for violin and viola. To avoid unison octaves, have the violinists play the "A" sections and the violists play the rest of the sections or vice versa. The only piece in Book Three which violists play and violinists do not is "Nina".

Two major points for the teacher of a combined violin and viola group to keep in mind are:

1. When playing low notes (especially on the C-string), violists need a generally slower bow speed than violinists'.

2. Violists (especially those who play on real violas and not violins-tuned-as-violas) use a wider and slower vibrato than violinists'.

**CENTRAL THEMES**

The teacher may wish to organize the Book Three group lesson time with a central theme such as those presented at the end of the Book Two chapter. Other possible themes are:
*Shifting*
*Vibrato*

**END OF LESSON**

As in the final time of earlier groups, the end of a Book Three lesson may include *solos*, the *Next-Piece game*, or *crazy treats*. A more difficult way to do the crazy treat of standing in a line and bowing neighbors' instruments is for one player to finger "May Song" while bowing "Twinkle Theme" on the instrument to his left.

# CHAPTER FIVE:
## SUZUKI BOOK FOUR

**INTRODUCTION**

Book Four students have learned many basics of using the instrument and bow, including shifting and vibrating. Suggestions for teaching students how to tune are found in the Book Two chapter introduction. Some may be able to tune by playing two strings at once as experienced players do. They must be careful to move only the peg or fine tuner of the string they are newly playing: for example, after tuning the A string, play D and A and now tune only the D. A perfectly-tuned fifth sounds "smooth", without "waves" or "beats".

Basic *warm-ups* include the "Twinkle" variations or a tonalization exercise. The teacher can plan the warm-ups to tie in with the group lesson emphasis of the day. Variations of Suzuki's basic tonalization exercise are in the introduction to the Book Three chapter. Book Four students can also play the basic tonalization exercise in second, third or fifth position.

**POSTURE**

All of the posture activities outlined in the Book Two chapter are pertinent to Book Four students:
- Awareness of feet and whole bodies
- Instrument hold
- Bow hold
- Relaxation exercises

**CONCENTRATION AND COORDINATION**

### 1. Memory Games

Memory games outlined in earlier chapters of this book are still appropriate.

### 2. Identification Games

Book Four students should be able to give the proper *full titles* of the pieces they play. The first piece in Book Four is often called "The First Seitz" but is actually "Concerto No. 2, 3rd movement, by Seitz". The students should understand that someone whose last name was Vivaldi wrote a concerto of which they learn the first and third movements in Book Four. Bring pictures of composers to show the students.

Have the students *identify snippets* of music which others play. Continue to identify *basic sections* of pieces learned earlier. A Book Four group should remember the Martini "Gavotte" well enough to play the B, C, D, and E sections in reverse order. Continue to label *pulse patterns* and *musical terms*.

Have the students sing the *pitch intervals* they are identifying. Someday they may be able to sing:

C      D      Major      second.      C      E      Major      third.      *etc.*

### 3. Antiphony

The "solo" and "tutti" sections of Vivaldi concerto movements are ideal for antiphony and give the students a feel for the contrasts built in to the design of the piece. A simple way to show these sections is for the teacher to stand with the group for the tutti sections and step forward and play alone during the solo sections. As a next step, the teacher has one student play with her during the solo sections. Eventually a different student can perform each solo section.

To make antiphonal rows more of a challenge, hold up one finger for the first row, two for the second row, etc., to signal who plays. If the teacher holds up fingers for which there is no row (for instance, if there are only four rows and the teacher holds up five fingers), the students all just hear the piece in their heads and resume playing when signalled.

### 4. Passage Work

Work on some difficult passages through first playing the underlying structural notes of the passage. In the first movement of Vivaldi's "Concerto in a minor" ("Concerto in d minor" for violists), practice measures 65-68 the following ways:

"Hiccups" and "doubles" continue to serve well in drilling difficult passages such as this one beginning with measure 75 of the third movement of Vivaldi's "Concerto in a minor" ("d minor"):

Many difficult spots need a lot of simple *repetition.* This can be done at the group lesson to demonstrate its effectiveness. If one or two students are still careless, have each student *play the difficult spot alone.*

After forewarning the students that a certain passage will be checked, set up a "*jail*" situation. Each student plays the passage; if he makes a mistake he must "go to jail" by sitting down. After everyone has had a turn, the jailbirds can try again to get out of jail. Be careful not to let this get negative.

To make sure that a sixteenth note passage with slurs is played with even rhythms, have some of the students play the passage without slurs while others play it as written.

## 5. Challenging "Twinkle"

To test how well Book Four students know the names of the notes they play, do "Twinkle" in octaves:

## 6. Relaxing Facial Muscles

If any of the students are plagued by grimaces or facial twitches while playing, have the entire class try to play a piece with their mouths open or while smiling. Another jaw relaxation aid is to touch the tip of the tongue to the roof of one's closed mouth.

## *RIGHT HAND TECHNIQUES*

### 1. Basic Down and Up, With Articulations

Separating the functions of the right and left hands is an important practice tool for players of all levels. *Shadow bowing* (as described in the Book One chapter) is still pertinent for introducing and reinforcing spots at a Book Four group lesson.

### 2. Bow Arm

Ways to control different *bow speeds, bow distribution,* and the *entire bow* are presented in the Book Three chapter.

*String crossings* reach a climax in Book Four with bariolage passages such as:

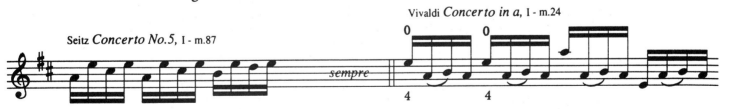

To practice such passages, have the students play without using their left hands. Then they can concentrate entirely on what their bow arms do:

If anyone tends to "shimmy" with his hips while playing a bariolage passage, have the students all stand on one leg while playing.

### 3. Tone

Book Four students continue to work for a good, firm sound on all four strings using each section of the bow. They try to control their *contact points*, use *natural arm weight*, and think of the bow hair *wrapping* around the string. Show them the importance of playing to the *bouts* of the instrument. When playing on the lower two strings, play toward the left side of the instrument. (This activates the bass bar more.) When playing on the upper two strings, play toward the right side of the instrument. (This activates the sound post more.)

To learn where a solid tone begins, practice "*garbage*" playing: use so much arm weight that a horrible crunching sound is produced. Can they do this all the way up the bow? Can anyone stand to listen to this?! This is analogous to a ship sinking under the water. In normal playing, the ship (bow) rides smoothly in the water.

*LEFT HAND TECHNIQUES*

### 1. Fingers

Some students have hands formed so that they will not touch the base of their first fingers to the neck of the instument when they play. Others (with small hands) may lightly touch the neck. The basic principle is *if you touch, don't clutch*; clutching at the base of the first finger creates difficulties in shifting and vibrating. To loosen left thumbs, slightly slide the thumb up and down the neck while playing a finger pattern such as: 0 1 2 3 4 3 2 1 0.

Clutching the instrument may be rooted in an insecure hold. A different chinrest may be of help, and the group lesson provides a good opportunity for trying out the variety of chinrests found on each others' instruments.

As begun at earlier-level groups, continue to practice finger patterns by playing *scales* as well as *familiar pieces in new keys and positions*. Add an extra mental challenge to scales: play with different numbers of steady notes per pitch (seven on the first pitch and one on the next pitch, for example). Also have the group play scales *skipping intervals* of a third, fourth, fifth, etc.

The "*Twisty Finger*" exercise is valuable for left-hand fingers. This exercise is called the "Woodie Waddie" exercise by John Kendall and is used here with his permission:

Try with 2 - 3, 3 - 4, 1 - 3, 2 - 4, and 1 - 4

When done at a group lesson, this exercise resembles sound effects from a science fiction movie!

## 2. Shifting

Early shifting exercises are in the Book Two and Three chapters of this book. A more-difficult version of the "Target Shifting Song" involves shifting with the "*old" finger to a new position:*

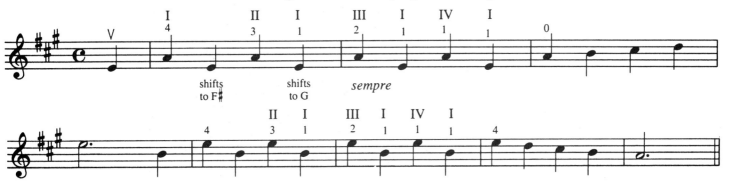

Have the group keep score of in-tune notes in this exercise, as described in the Book Three chapter.

Try playing "Chorus" with a shift to a new position on each phrase.

There are several shifts in the Book Four literature (and some in the Viola Book Three pieces) which involve "old finger-new position". One prime example occurs in the first movement of Vivaldi's "Concerto in a minor" ("d minor"), when the first finger (the "old" finger) should practice shifting to third position, though the note actually sounded next in the piece will be fourth finger:

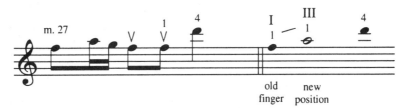

Some call the shift-practice note a "ghost" note as it is present but unheard.

## 3. Harmonics

In addition to playing the "Target Shifting Song" with harmonics (see the Book Two chapter), challenge the students to play "Reveille" with harmonics:

### 4. Vibrato

Vibrato exercises are in the Book Two and Book Three chapters. If those exercises are under control, let the students use their bows at the same time they try to vibrate with the left hand. Try a slow-motion vibrato to the words of "pizza" (vibrato speed of two eighth notes) and "pepperoni" (speed of four sixteenth notes). Try a *tap and hold* exercise:

Try to vibrate during review pieces such as "Chorus". To stimulate faster vibrato, try *vibrating while playing with a tremolo bow.*

Always vibrate when playing with the class so that the students have a good visual image of vibrato.

## MUSICALITY

As first discussed in the Book Two chapter, dynamics, ensemble skills, and awareness of what is fitting together to make the whole piece are central elements of helping students play musically. They must exaggerate what is different. They use many different *registers* of their instruments and are capable of bringing out a variety of *timbres.*

### 1. Direction of Line

Moving lines get more complex in Book Four literature. In the third movement of Vivaldi's "Concerto in a minor" ("d minor" for violists), the bariolage section contains an obvious moving line:

m. 111

The final works of both violin and viola Book Four are double concertoes. Here the player with the more static part must back off and listen to the other player's moving line:

Bach *Concerto in d for 2 Violins*, I - m. 32

*Give direction to repeated notes and figures.* The repeated notes in the opening of Vivaldi's "Concerto in a minor" ("d minor" for violists) become exciting if done with a crescendo:

Vivaldi *Concerto in a*, I

Later in the same work, another crescendo makes the repeated figure much more interesting:

Vivaldi *Concerto in a*, I - m.7

*crescendo*

## 2. Character

Build awareness of composers' instructions as to the *character* of pieces. For example, the third movement of Seitz' "Concerto No. 2" is marked "grazioso", "espressivo e tranquillo", "brillante", and "risoluto" in different sections. These words are close enough to English to be intelligible to Book Four students. Go back to earlier pieces to practice some characters; "The Two Grenadiers" has a strong "risoluto" section.

**CENTRAL THEMES**

The teacher may wish to organize the Book Four group lesson time with a central theme such as those listed at the end of the Book Three chapter.

**END OF LESSON**

As in the final time of earlier groups, the end of a Book Four lesson may include *solos*, the "*Next-Piece game*", or a *crazy treat*.

# BIRTHDAYS

## Composers and Performers
## Selected by Suzuki for learning
## Violin and Viola Books 1-4

### January
4 - Pergolesi
17 - Gossec
20 - Fiocco
31 - Schubert

### February
2 - Kreisler
19 - Boccherini
23 - Handel

### March
4 - Vivaldi
14 - Telemann
21 - J.S. Bach

### April
24 - Martini

### May
7 - Brahms
11 - Becker

### June
8 - Schumann
12 - Seitz

### July

### August
5 - Thomas
23 - Primrose

### September
8 - Dvorak

### October
17 - Suzuki
27 - Paganini

### November
27 - Lully

### December
16 - Beethoven
29 - Casals